Handmade Lace & Patterns

Books by Annette Feldman

KNIT, PURL, AND DESIGN!
CROCHET AND CREATIVE DESIGN
BEGINNER'S NEEDLECRAFT
HANDMADE LACE & PATTERNS

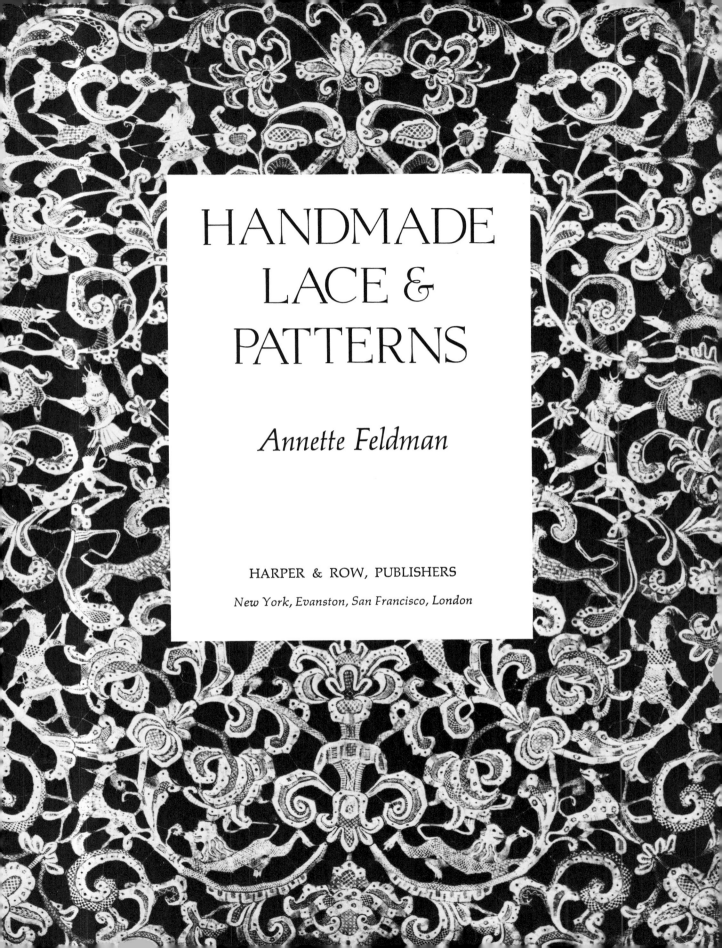

HANDMADE LACE & PATTERNS

Annette Feldman

HARPER & ROW, PUBLISHERS

New York, Evanston, San Francisco, London

All stitch directions in this book have been thoroughly checked for accuracy. We cannot, however, be responsible for misinterpretation of directions or variations caused by the individual's working techniques.

FIRST EDITION

Designed by Janice Willcocks Stern

―――――――――――――――――――

Library of Congress Cataloging in Publication Data

Feldman, Annette.
   Handmade lace and patterns.
   Bibliography: p.
   Includes index.
   1. Lace and lace making.   2. Lace and lace making—
     making—
Patterns. I. Title.
TT800.F44 1975   746.2   74–1806
ISBN 0–06–011231–X

―――――――――――――――――――

75 76 77 78 79 10 9 8 7 6 5 4 3 2 1

Dedicated to my parents, Gertrude and Emanuel Gerber
my husband, Irving
and to Ronnie and Melanie Marks, and
Jennifer Lamont, and Mark Feiner
and John and Justin Lamont

CONTENTS

PART I

The Story of Lace

1 From Primitive Nets to the Glorious Beauty of Fine Lace   3

The history of the gradual yet very definite progress of the lace-making art from primitive man's earliest experimentation with the knotting and netting of several strands of coarse natural fiber to the making, centuries later, of exquisitely fine needlepoint and bobbin laces. The road is carefully coursed and each step along the way is recorded in detail. Methods for making filet, drawnwork, and cutwork are described, as well as those for needlerun pieces and, among many others, the beautiful Carrickmacross of Ireland.

2 Many Loved Lace in Many Ways   27

A romance of lace, telling of how it was loved by many, each in his own way. Stories of early Egyptians and their neighbors reveal how they enjoyed the addition of decorative finery to otherwise drab clothing; how the clergy found the white, airy purity of the texture of lace symbolic of the beauty and spirit of God; how Renaissance noblemen vied for possession of it as a status symbol; and how even Napoleon, the fearsome warrior, loved delicate lace to a passion and went to great extremes to buy it for his own personal use and for the pleasure of those around him.

3 Lace-Making Around the World   52

An imaginary journey through many of the lace centers of the world, some important for their contribution to the actual evolvement of the various lace-making techniques; others for being the pacesetters for the use of lace in fashion; and still others for their ethnic interest. The background for how and why each developed in its own way is analyzed, and we learn about the magnificent point de Venise laces of Italy, the Mechlin and Binche pieces of Flanders, the Alençons and Argentans of France and, among several more, the point d'Espagne, the English Honiton and the Irish Youghal laces.

PART II

Patterns

4 Edgings, Insertions, and Motifs   95

A collection of trimming designs to be made with some of the implements used in lace work today. There are crocheted pieces and knitted ones, and some that are made with a tatting shuttle. Designs are shown in which an edging, an insert, and a group of motifs have been used as the very important component parts of a beautiful whole, and suggestions are given as to how the traditional designs may be varied by those who wish to achieve a more contemporary look in their work.

Preface

The story of lace-making from its crude beginnings, the many ways in which lace was used, and the great peak to which it ascended in both beauty and popularity is a very fascinating one indeed. Lace has ever been a source of delight as a form of decorative finery, and the esteem held for it in the minds and hearts of many is perhaps best described in a letter written to Boswell by the erudite Dr. Samuel Johnson in 1728. Making a comparison to what was deemed in those days to be the ultimate in knowledge, he said: "Greek, Sir, is like lace; every man gets as much of it as he can." With a less terse approach, a Mrs. Thomas Ellis Baker, who lived in the nineteenth century, described her own love for lace poetically:

> Let me grow lovely growing old,
> So many fine things do.
> Laces and ivory and gold
> And silks need not be new.

Although this beautiful art of embellishment started early in the time of man, it took many centuries and many stages of development in both method and style until in the reign of King Louis XIV of France the making of true lace reached its epitome of beauty and perfection. It was then that the love and appreciation for it became so great, and the desire to possess it so intense that many treasured it more than money, and often preferred it to other available currencies as a medium of payment. A fine piece was often worth in those days a price commensurate only with the desire on the part of some individual to own it, and some of the prices were indeed high.

Today precious old pieces have become a valued art form, as important to lace collectors as are fine antiques and paintings to those who deal in these art forms. Most of our great museums and many interested individuals own priceless and irreplaceable collections of fine lace—treasured ecclesiastical altar pieces and vestments, old tablecloths and bedspreads, many smaller pieces made for personal adornment, and small bits and fragments of other larger pieces, the better part of which had perhaps worn away with the passing of time. Often the smaller pieces are carefully mounted under glass, while at other times they are arranged on velvet trays much resembling those used for the display of precious jewels. Most of the pieces are further preserved with parchment coverings to protect them from dust and other elements which might tend to disintegrate the fragile threads from which they were made.

To collectors and those who are most knowledgeable on the subject of lace-making, there are only two true types, the needlepoint and the pillow or bobbin laces, and these, being the rarest and finest of all, are also the most priceless and precious ones in existence today. Included among these beautiful varieties are the magnificent Alencon and gros point de Venise needlepoint pieces, and the handsome Valenciennes and Chantilly bobbin laces.

Other fine old pieces also exist, among these the exquisite needlerun and Carrickmacross laces, treasured and esteemed by connoisseurs, but just a little less important in value since these, though lovely indeed, were worked on fine machine-made net backgrounds, in contrast to the true laces which were completely made by hand. There are, too, the lovely old knitted and tatted and crocheted laces and those which are made of macramé. Very beautiful forms of handwork, many of them are counted among the collectors' store of wealth, but again they are of still lesser value to the purists who consider them rather crude forms of the art, developed by methods and techniques far more simple than those involved in the making of the finer pieces.

Until now we have referred to lace as a collector's item, and to the making of it as practically a lost art. Basically this is true, particularly when we refer to the beautiful needlepoint and bobbin laces. The making of these requires an amount of patience and skill far exceeding those of most people today, other than perhaps just a relatively few in convents and isolated communities who still carry on this type of work, and a few others who do yet try the classic old methods, claiming that the slow, painstaking work and the immeasurable amount of dexterity required imparts to them the spiritual comfort and rewarding inner satisfaction that can come only to those who are creating a true work of art.

Experts tell us that the deftness of hand that is needed for the making of fine lace can only be acquired by those who are most dedicated to the art and who are willing to practice it from an early age and with the same diligence and endeavor as one who might be studying to be a ballet dancer or a very fine musician. History bears out this claim: at the height of the great lace-making era during the

Golden Age of the Renaissance in Middle Europe very young children were selected to be trained in the art, and we know, too, that little girls became expert lace-makers by the time they had reached the age of 13, having acquired by then an incredible nimbleness in their work.

As every rule has its exception, however, one of the few unusual ones relating to the making of true lace in modern times is the operation of the small but rather important industry existing in Belgium today, its revival having begun during the days of World War I. The priceless skill of making fine lace had managed somehow to survive there through the centuries, having been kept alive by a number of enterprising businessmen who took advantage of that country's great production of flax, the raw natural fiber so important for the making of fine linen thread, of the lace-making knowledge of the few remaining older artisans, and of poor young girls, who were offered a pittance to learn the art and were further exploited by being paid very little for their labor and effort in carrying it on.

During the war, the invading enemy were quick to appraise the value of the existing lace industry and were willing to trade amnesty for the workers, who absolutely refused to sell either their knowledge or their skill for any price. Defeated in their purpose, the invaders proceeded to destroy everything connected in any way with the lace-making industry that they could not take over. The valuable flax crops in the Valley of Lys were devastated, mills were demolished, and the entire city of Ypres, an important lace center, was wiped out.

After the war, when the government attempted to help the war victims, attention was belatedly focused on the plight of the destitute lace workers, and on the poor conditions that had existed among them for many years prior to the war. Queen Elizabeth, with the aid of the church, made special effort then to pull the industry together again, and through their combined efforts, the Brussels Lace Committee was formed. Trade agreements were made with England whereby that country supplied thread for the lace-makers, and agreed to buy back the lace that was to be made of the thread. The church opened its doors for the use of new model lace-making schools, where former victims could find work and where young children, following the old tradition, were again trained in the art. It is this group of young children, schooled at that time, who are still carrying on the great art of making fine handmade lace in Belgium, and who comprise perhaps the largest group of such workers in the world today.

Unfortunately, and too typical of much that has happened during the so-called progress of time and civilization, the coming of the Machine Age at the start of the nineteenth century saw the beginning of the end of the practice of many of the handcrafts, including the making of the beautiful needlepoint and bobbin laces. The Industrial Revolution ushered in new machines capable of producing the fine net backgrounds over which lace patterns could be worked. This was the beginning of the making of the needlerun and Carrickmacross laces. Before too many years had passed, machines were developed that were capable of producing not only background nets, but also lace in which all handwork was eliminated, thus duplicating many of the lace patterns worked over the nets.

With this new technology lace could be made more quickly, and consequently at a comparatively much lower cost. As time went on the demand for the new, cheaper machine-made lace rose sharply while that for the handmade or partially handmade pieces declined to the point where the practice of making them became practically nonexistent. Gradually the art became a lost one, and the older handmade pieces were relegated to the files of the collectors.

The inventor of the first lace-making machine was an Englishman, a Mr. Hammond. His 1768 machine was finally perfected by 1798 after much experimentation, and at that time the first real production of net began in England. Many from other countries that were interested in the lace industry were impressed with the new machines and the new methods and were eager to import the techniques.

Lace-makers in France were particularly interested, but met with strong obstacles in their efforts to obtain the knowledge they wanted. France and England were at war, and in addition to the English reluctance to share their prized invention, there was the problem also of circumventing Napoleon's forbiddance of trade or contact with the enemy. Not until the power of Napoleon began to wane was someone finally able to smuggle the first of the English machines into France, and it was just a few years later, when Napoleon was beleaguered with his own problems of exile, that the great French machine-made lace industry came into its own, the industry for which the English were the innovators, their mechanical skill, however, needing the creative imagination of the French to bring it into prominence.

The making of good machine lace is an art in itself, and some of the work that the French people developed was, and is yet today, very fine indeed. Although there are a few stitches which can only be imitated but not really duplicated by machine, such as the simple buttonhole stitch used in the making of handmade lace, or the *cordonnet* (buttonhole-upon-buttonhole) stitch raised effect, other laces can be beautifully made, whether copies or original in design. These are much in demand now, and fine pieces are quite costly. Interesting, too, is the fact that Cluny and Alençon and other areas in France so renowned through the centuries for their magnificent handmade laces are the very same great lace-making centers so famous today for their lovely machine-made pieces. An explanation for this is that the workers in these areas were already highly skilled in their art, and the transferring of their basic skill to the one involved in the making of machine-made lace was rather a simple matter.

As we follow the history of lace, we want to tell you all about lace of every type, and to relate many interesting tales, starting with the one about how primitive man's knotting two vines together was the very beginning of the making, centuries later, of the most unimaginably beautiful laces, and going on to the time of the peak of the lace-making era in Europe when the craze and desire to possess lace reached such ridiculous extremes that the industry became a very important social and economic factor in the lives of the people. An example of this was the custom of wealthy lords and ladies during the extravagant reign of King Louis XV of France of vying with each other in the elegance of their morning bathroom reception, a ceremony during which the host or hostess reclined in a tub full of water (discreetly clouded and perfumed!), with the tub as well as the walls, towels, mats, and other linens in their bathrooms completely decorated with flounce upon flounce of very fine lace. Many stories are told about how far the extremes went, and the extent to which people put themselves out in those days to satisfy their passion for lace, and to fulfill the whims of insatiable aristocrats.

Another tale that is rather unusual and very indicative of the frenzied passion for lace, is the one that has often been told about the smuggling of lace from one country to another in a most ingenious way, the job being done on the backs of starving dogs. Laces were being made in Flanders that simply could not be copied in any way in France, and because these laces could not be duplicated in France and because, too, there simply could never be enough fine lace to satisfy all the desires of all the people, French noblemen went to ridiculous lengths to be able to secure as much of it as they possibly could. Flemish mercenaries were encouraged by French merchants and helped to smuggle packet upon packet of very fine lace.

The arrangement was worked by smugglers and dealers in the border towns of the two countries, and involved the use of dogs as the unassuming illegal messengers for the valuable running trade between the two countries. Dogs were raised on the French side of the border where they were pampered and given the most luxurious of treatment. Plump, satisfied, and well fed, they were then delivered to Flanders where half of them were starved and badly mistreated, and the remainder of them were given the same luxurious treatment that they had had in France. Woe unto the well-fed dogs, however, for when the poor starved creatures became lean and bony, their backs were padded with packets containing several strips of precious lace, and then covered with the hides of the dogs who had been allowed to remain fat for just that very purpose. The so-called "messengers" were then turned loose with the contraband goods on their backs. Their first and most natural instinct was to run as fast as they could back to the happy homes they had come from, and away from the place where they had been so badly treated. Having made it across the border, they were immediately seized by the French conspirators, who removed the valuable packets and delivered their contents for fabulous sums to their many French compatriots who were beside themselves with joy to have possession of the precious strips of beautiful Brussels lace.

We will also describe the very interesting ways in which many of the beautiful old laces were made, and show photographs depicting the various methods that were used in their making, and additional photographs showing you the styles to which the laces were adapted, including copies of several famous museum paintings in which lace was an important part of the costume of the day. We will tell about all the great lace-making centers of the world, and show you many examples of the type of work for which each was best known.

Finally, we will talk about the kinds of lace that are still being made by hand today, no longer indeed the very fine work which reached its peak at the beginning of the nineteenth century, but nevertheless beautiful types of embellishing adornment, and very symbolic of the late twentieth century in which we live. We will show you many pictures of the interesting things we are making, and we will tell you exactly how you can go about making these things for yourself, lovely things which perhaps collectors centuries later will admire as our own particular contribution to the art of handmade lace, beautifully styled, well-fashioned, and so much a story of our time.

PART I

The Story of Lace

ONE

From Primitive Nets to the Glorious Beauty of Fine Lace

In the Kircheriano Museum in Rome are very ancient knotted game bags and nets, primitive man's ingenious invention for catching wild beasts, a thought which had perhaps come to him from his earliest experimentation with the knotting together of two, and then three and four, vines. It is also known from archeological research that primitive man had learned that by the knotting together of several strands of coarse natural fibers he could fashion strong, sturdy nets with which to catch the fish that swam in the rivers and streams. Those early men who lived close to the seacoast quickly learned too that larger and stronger nets could haul in for them a very rich catch from the sea. There could have been no thought in the minds of either the game hunter or the fisherman of those early days that the crude type of openwork mesh he had so cleverly devised for his own

very basic needs would become, with the passage of time, the important forerunner of one of our world's finest artistic achievements —the making of the magnificent needlepoint and bobbin laces which attained such great glory centuries later, during the Golden Age of the Renaissance in Europe.

There were, of course, many steps in the transition from the primitive game and fish nets to the making of fine lace. Early man, as he used nets he made, realized quickly that those coarse utilitarian pieces that served him as a means of survival could, if made of a finer material, be used as some sort of embellishment for the very simple dress he wore. He began to experiment with other, more delicate fibers, and with different ways of knotting the strands together. He learned, too, that the fine strong fibers he was using could be woven together to create a crude type of fabric which could be fashioned into clothing, and that with the borders of the fabric fringed or knotted in the manner of his earlier nets, he could have a rather attractive garment for himself. He also realized that just fine nets themselves could be decorated with shiny shells, stones, or flowers and be used as personal adornment. The use of openwork material as a form of ornamentation soon became established.

The art of lace-making in the Middle East progressed gradually from this very early beginning to a position of some importance. Very definite references to the art are found in the writings of the Old Testament itself. In Exodus, the second book of the Bible, it is evident that embroidery was used to a large extent in the time of Moses. In Isaiah III:23 there is a pronouncement of woe from the prophet on the Egyptians, who valued fine ornamentation above more godly pursuits; and the writings of Ezekiel speak clearly of both Syrian and Egyptian embroidery. Although it is true that the interesting darned nets and fringes that appear on the old Babylonian sculptures of Nineveh bear little resemblance to the magnificently worked laces of later centuries, nevertheless the value of this work in the history of lace-making should not be underestimated.

It was such efforts as these in the direction of using various types of openwork fabric as a form of decorative finery that ultimately culminated in the creation of fine lace as we have known it for the past few centuries and as we know it today. Ancient Egypt soon took a giant step forward in the cultivation of its new art. The people were inspired by the adaptability of the art and were encouraged to go on by the ready availability of the rich flax crops from the fertile Valley of the Nile which supplied them with the fine thread they needed. Applying the existing practical knowledge of net-making of the seacoast habitants, they worked on many interesting variations of this type of net, elaborating new patterns with different kinds of glass beads and little gold ornaments, placed within the openings of their knotted mesh. Pleased with what they had done, and stimulated then with the knowledge that their clothing could be made really beautiful, they also found new ways to fringe and knot the hems of their linen garments, and in this way to fashion many attractive new designs.

The ancient Egyptians learned, too, to draw out the threads from the body of the fabric itself and to work decorative motifs, perhaps with colored or gold thread, over the vertical threads that remained. They experimented with many ways of refining and improving upon the fascinating work they were doing, and they were very proud indeed of the net veils and scarfs and headdresses that were worn by Egypt's royal ladies, some pieces of which have been discovered, miraculously preserved, in fifth- to sixth-century Egypto-Roman tombs.

Network cap, made of undyed wool. Egyptian (Coptic), fifth or sixth century. The Metropolitan Museum of Art, New York (Purchase, 1889)

It is interesting to note that some bits of evidence have also been found that indicate quite conclusively that the bobbin technique of lace-making was known in those days. In the Cinquantenaire Museum at Brussels there is a photograph of a small linen bag, such as might be carried today, which was found in the tomb of the Priestess of Hathor in Egypt. The design of the bag leaves no doubt that it was made with bobbins, for the mesh it is made of is almost identical to the type used in the making of the more modern Valenciennes lace. Excavations in Claterna, an ancient Roman city near Bologna, have even unearthed a pair of bone bobbins which were found lying positioned exactly as such bobbins have always been used in the making of this kind of lace.

Network cap made of red wool and undyed linen. Egyptian (Coptic), fifth or sixth century. The Metropolitan Museum of Art, New York (Purchase, 1889)

Network cap made of brown linen. Egyptian (Coptic), fifth or sixth century. The Metropolitan Museum of Art, New York (Gift of George F. Baker, 1890)

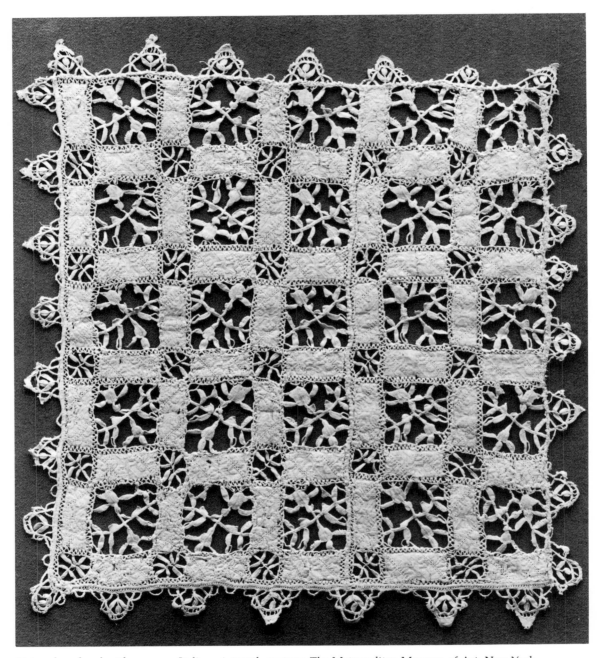

Cutwork and embroidery cover. Italian, sixteenth century. The Metropolitan Museum of Art, New York (Gift of Mrs. J. E. Spingarn, 1938)

It seems hardly a coincidence that before long, word of the lace-making skills developed in the ancient seaport towns of Egypt and Babylonia spread via the maritime traffic to the coastal towns in Europe, particularly to Venice in Italy and to the ancient Greek ports on the Aegean, and in some way on to the ports of Flanders too; and then from the ports into the more inland areas of the various countries. Early Latin writings describe trimmings for the *scultulata vestis*, a type of Roman toga, as being made with borders of reticulated weaving, a form of open mesh or net. The early variations of this work were made by ingeniously cutting open spaces on woven linen cloth, then placing threads over the open spaces in various directions to create a design, and working small, very tight buttonhole stitches over the threads to secure the design in place. This type of work is most definitely an early forerunner of the beautiful needlepoint laces, the making of which was to develop many years later.

The story of how each of the European countries advanced the art of lace-making through its own culture is a most interesting one. In Italy this art began during the fifteenth century and developed to its greatest height during the sixteenth. The early techniques of the cutwork that started in Egypt were advanced and further developed in Italy, as was drawnwork, known as *punto tirato*. In this type of lace-making threads are drawn from a piece of material and the design is worked with a fine needle and embroidery stitches over the remaining vertical threads.

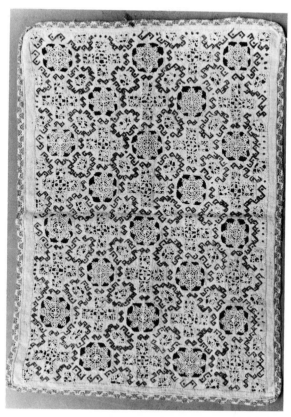

Cutwork cover. Italian, sixteenth century. The Metropolitan Museum of Art, New York (Gift of Mrs. Albert Blum, 1920)

While the Middle East is credited as having been the origin of this kind of work, it was in Italy that this art was truly refined. Many new and beautiful patterns were designed, although these new drawn-thread patterns were still not quite as rich and lavish in character as the Italian laces that were made later. The earlier work was rather geometric in character, since it was based always on the particular threads that were drawn from the material.

The art of decorated net lace-making, a very direct descendant of man's early fishnets, also flourished in Italy. The Egyptians had refined their early nets and had learned to darn in and out to create simple patterns and later to decorate these patterns with glass beads and other passimenterie. Now the Italians improved greatly upon this method by using very fine thread for their nets and then working over these threads with the finest of embroidery stitches, in this way forming a lace pattern known as *lacis*, or *filet*. A later development of this was *buratto*, the art of weaving the net on a loom.

Very often, too, during the growth of the lace-making industry in Italy, especially stunning effects were achieved by an artistic combining of the three different techniques in a single pattern.

That the progress of the art of lace-making was a gradual and quite natural one can best be exemplified by the fact that Italian cutwork, known as *punto tagliato*, was originally a type of embroidery. But, since dyes then known were not sufficiently fast and there was consequently the problem of their fad-

Drawnwork altar cloth. Italian-Sicilian, fifteenth century. The Metropolitan Museum of Art, New York (Rogers Fund, 1920)

ing in the sun or in the course of being washed, the embroidery needed always to be worked with white thread on white cloth. This resulted in a rather monotonous look which did not at all please the Italian workers, and they soon devised the idea of cutting out the material within the embroidered designs, thus achieving a very light, airy, and handsome finished piece of lace.

It was from this method of working the design on the material first, then cutting out the open spaces within the design to create the desired lacy effect, that another method developed, that of cutting out the open spaces in the material first and then working around and across the spaces. This was done by throwing threads across the open spaces in either direction and then buttonhole-stitching tightly over the threads. This technique produced a very attractive and popular type of lace, geometric in pattern and known as *reticello*, the name which later became the generic term for all lace of geometric design.

Eventually clever workers experimented with dispensing with the basic material altogether, and simply working over threads fastened to a surface in a chosen design. Thus, from embroidery to cutwork to reticello came

Drawnwork band. Crimson silk on linen. Italian, sixteenth century. The Metropolitan Museum of Art, New York (Gift of Ruth and Gordon Washburn, 1962)

Drawnwork panel with brown and white thread. Italian-Sicilian, sixteenth century. The Metropolitan Museum of Art, New York (Rogers Fund, 1920)

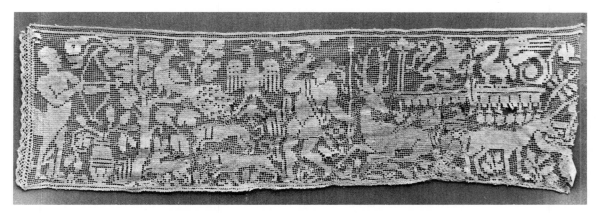

Buratto panel. Italian, early seventeenth century. The Metropolitan Museum of Art, New York (Gift by subscription, 1909. Blackborne Collection)

finally the first of the needlepoint laces, *punto in aria*—"point in the air." It was thus named because it was worked, literally, in the air, free of any cloth foundation or confining background. Although the style of this type of lace was a little stiff to start with, as needle workers gradually became more aware of the design possibilities of this new method, the patterns became more graceful and finally evolved into such rich and gracefully flowing forms as the famous Venetian rose point, one of the most beautiful and elegant laces ever made.

It is interesting to note that the word *punto* as used in *punto tagliato, punto tirato*, and *punto in aria*—or *point*, as in *point de Brussels* and *point d'Alençon*—means "prick," and refers to the initial pricking with a fine needle on parchment of whatever pattern is to be worked. It is a way of starting to work all the needlepoint laces and some of the bobbin lace, the other true lace (to be described later), the making of which also involves the basic design being initially pricked with a fine needle on paper.

To return to the story of the development of lace-making in Italy and to the innovative method of *punto in aria*, it was by using this method that the Italians were able to create many glorious new needlepoint patterns, most of which are characterized by the rich, lavish effects so typical of the temperament and taste of the Italian personality. Included among them are the glorious gros point de Venise and the plat de Venise laces.

In Chapter 3, which describes lace-making centers throughout the world, many of these very fine Italian lace designs will be described in detail and shown in photographs. There will also be descriptions of different types of lace from other renowned centers which sprang up and flourished as the years went on. Many types of lace will be discussed in that chapter, and to the newcomer to the art of lace-making it will probably be a little bewildering to read the many names given to the varieties of lace that have been made in the different parts of the world. And in one particular case there was even a lace that was made in one area and named after another—

Lacis panel. Italian, sixteenth or early seventeenth century. Victoria and Albert Museum, London (Crown Copyright)

Reticello border. Italian, mid-sixteenth century. Cooper-Hewitt Museum of Decorative Arts and Design, Smithsonian Institution, New York (Ex coll. Baroness Kisch)

Borders of reticello and needlepoint. Italian, sixteenth or early seventeenth century. Victoria and Albert Museum, London (Crown Copyright)

that of point d'Angleterre, which was a fine variety of lace made in Brussels, not in England. It was given that name for reasons a little obscure in themselves, some saying that it was so named because it was made of English thread, others saying that it was made for export to England, and for political reasons, its point of origin was not to be known. Actually, there never have been as many varieties as there have been names for laces; it is the great overlapping of many names for practically the same kinds of lace that creates the confusion.

Many laces, whether needle- or bobbin-made, are actually very similar to one another, but as time went on, some towns imitated the laces of other areas and other towns developed a few special characteristics of their own. In many instances, when the pattern was imitated, a new name, most likely the name of the town where the lace was made, was given to the work. In other instances where a few new characteristics were added to the design, a totally new name was given.

To collectors of lace this presents rather a problem, particularly in the case of those laces which have been imitated. The responsibility is upon the buyer to establish the authenticity of a particular piece, this being determined

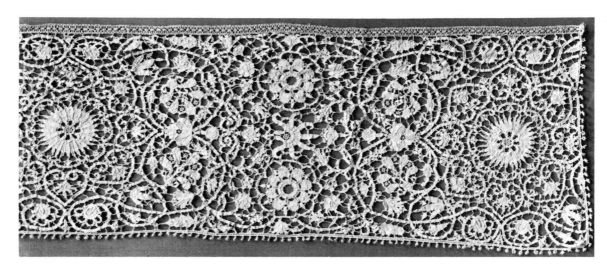

Punto in aria border. Italian, early seventeenth century. The Metropolitan Museum of Art, New York (Gift by subscription, 1909. Blackborne Collection)

largely by the quality of the workmanship and the color and fineness of the thread that was used.

Before we go on to the story of the development and making of bobbin or pillow lace, the other true lace whose development occurred almost simultaneously with that of needlepoint lace and which is known by the name of either of the materials used—a number of bobbins and a hard-stuffed pillow —it should be of interest to know the basic way in which most of the fine needlepoint laces were actually made.

A pattern was first picked, then copied onto drawing paper and tacked onto a drawing board, next tracing paper tacked over it, and the design transferred to the tracing paper. A piece of unglazed black paper was then tacked under the tracing, and the design was trans-

Gros point de Venise border. Italian, seventeenth century. The Metropolitan Museum of Art, New York (Gift by subscription, 1909. Blackborne Collection)

ferred to the paper by pricking through it with a fine needle or pin, placing the marks approximately ⅜ inch apart. The black paper was then tacked or basted to two layers of strong cotton or linen material, and the design was outlined by sewing three lengths of white thread through the pricked holes and the underlying material, which was eventually cut away when the design was completed and the backing was removed. The lace was then made by working with a series of fine buttonhole stitches within the outlined spaces. When the piece of lace was completed, the layers were cut apart with a sharp knife slipped between them, severing the outlining stitches so that the finished piece could be easily pulled off. The principle of making this kind of lace was indeed quite simple, but the work needed to be very carefully done and with a great deal of skill and patience because of its fineness and precision.

We have described the gradual development of the making of fine needlepoint lace and told of the various early techniques involved in the art. We have preferred to describe this type of work first, rather than bobbin lace, the other true type, for two reasons. The first is that needlepoint lace seems to have always been held in just a little higher esteem because the delicate fabric is created with nothing more than a needle and a length of very fine thread, this in contrast to bobbin lace, the making of which requires the aid of a tool. The second reason is that the history of the needlepoint art is more directly traceable. In contrast, the development of pillow or bobbin lace is a bit vague, and while we know that it, too, was an ancient

"The Lacemaker." The National Gallery of Art, Washington, D.C. (Andrew Mellon Collection)

Macramé. Italian, late sixteenth or early seventeenth century. Cooper-Hewitt Museum of Decorative Arts and Design, Smithsonian Institution, New York (Ex coll. Richard C. Greenleaf)

art, whether the start of its major development occurred in Italy or in Flanders is not accurately known. Generally, however, and we do agree, it is felt that the people of Flanders should be credited with the growth and refinement of this particular art, and for being responsible for the finest pieces made. The delicacy and minuteness of many of the designs are more in keeping with the temperament of the Flemish, and rather different from those of the Italians whose easier and freer personalities wanted and were capable of creating bolder and more flowing patterns.

While history does not actually tell us too many consecutive facts about the early development of bobbin lace, fantasy does offer us one rather charming tale about it. According to the legend, the beginning of bobbin lace-making was in Flanders, and this distinctive technique was first conceived of by a young girl named Serena who was adept at needlework and lived very long ago in the city of Bruges. As the story goes, one day Serena was sitting under a tree in the courtyard of her home, quietly praying for some miracle to provide her the means for caring for her dying mother, and, even as she prayed, a perfectly formed spider web fell onto the black apron that covered her lap. She felt that this was the answer to her prayer, and rising carefully, she gently removed her apron, took up her needle and thread and tried to copy the beautiful, dainty, fragile net of the web.

Primitive Nets to the Glorious Beauty of Fine Lace **17**

As she worked, however, her threads became tangled, and as she sat wondering what to do next, her lover appeared and, hearing of her dilemma, suggested that she tie each of the separate strands she was using to a twig, which could serve as a handle or weight and thus prevent the many threads from becoming tangled. Serena did as her lover suggested, and she was at once successful in being able to work her threads, and shortly thereafter to reproduce the design of the lovely spider web. This, so the tale claims, was the very start of the making of bobbin lace in Flanders, an art which Serena went on to teach to many others in her country.

The story is rather a charming one, and although this book relies on fact and not fancy, we would still credit the progress of this particular art to Flanders, rather than to Italy, for it was in Flanders that the skill of making bobbin lace really progressed to a point of peak perfection. We say this in spite of being aware that, just as *punto tagliato* and *punto tirato* are considered the direct forerunners of needlepoint lace, so many believe that *punto groppo*, the art of knotting generally identified by its Moorish name of macramé, bears a definite relationship to the making of bobbin lace and that this art was practiced in early days in convents in Milan where a great deal of it was made for use as coverings for church furniture. The difference between the two crafts is that macramé is a heavier type of work, generally done with thick cord, while the similarity between them

is that in both instances the construction and design of the lace depends primarily on the manipulation of many individual threads.

As the various knottings became more elaborate and the threads more exquisitely fine in the design of bobbin-lace pieces, so it became more important to find tools such as bobbins around which one could wind the various threads. It is interesting to note that the making of bobbin lace is really just a form of plaiting, and there are, in the making of most varieties of this lace, only two simple movements. It is the way in which these two movements are combined and the variation in the number of pairs of bobbins used that give each type of lace its particular style and character.

Our lady Serena's bobbins were fashioned of twigs but others were made of bone, this being the reason why bobbin lace is sometimes referred to as bone lace. Still other bobbins were made of wood; actually, bobbins could be made of any other moderately strong holding material.

The pillow used in making this kind of lace came in various forms. A round pillow, by far the more popular type, was most frequently used for making the so-called free laces—*fils coupés*—a type of work done in separate small pieces and then joined together. Included in this group of laces are many of the most artistic Flemish pieces, for it was in using this method that workers were able to achieve some of the free artistic effects generally credited to the designs of the finest

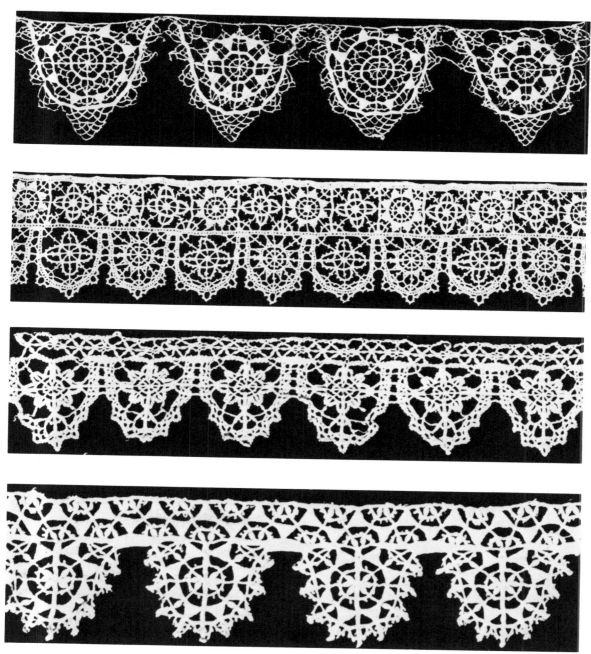

From top to bottom:

1. Reticello border. Origin unknown. Late sixteenth century
2. Reticello and bobbin lace strip. Band is made of reticello, and frame along bottom half is bobbin lace. Italian, late sixteenth century
3 and 4. Bobbin lace strips. Italian, late sixteenth or early seventeenth century
All of the above are from the Cooper-Hewitt Museum of Decorative Arts and Design, Smithsonian Institution, New York

Bobbin lace cravat. Brussels, early eighteenth century. Cooper-Hewitt Museum of Decorative Arts and Design, Smithsonian Institution, New York

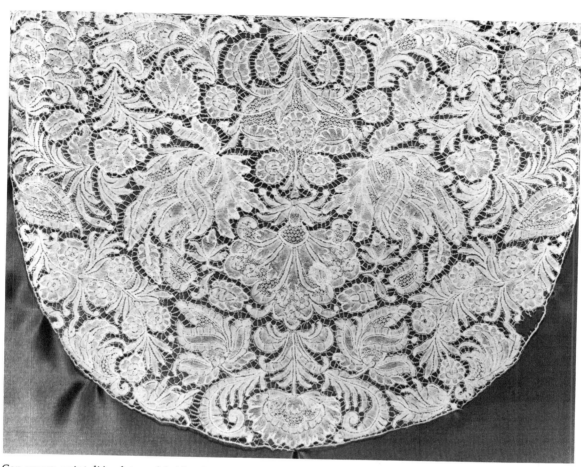

Cap crown, point d'Angleterre à brides. Brussels, early eighteenth century. Cooper-Hewitt Museum of Decorative Arts and Design, Smithsonian Institution, New York (Ex coll. Mrs. Robert B. Noyes)

needlepoint pieces. The most common form of pillow used for this type of work was a firmly stuffed one made of two pieces of strong material such as mattress ticking, each one about 13 to 15 inches in diameter and joined together by a band of the same material approximately 3 inches wide. One of the particular advantages of working with a round pillow of this kind was that one could turn it to accommodate the working of the pattern, even as the pattern was taking shape.

Pieces were small because they could never be larger than the pillow and no pillow would be large enough to make a bedspread or tablecloth. Therefore, any large item would need to be made of small pieces joined together. Again as to size, pieces could be made smaller than the pillow size. When a number of round-pillow lace pieces had been completed, the separate pieces were either joined to a mesh background, or *fond*, or put together with a series of *brides*, which are bars of connecting threads over which tight buttonhole stitches were worked. These brides formed an important part of any particular lace pattern and were often themselves decorated in some way, usually with *picots* or tiny pearl-like embellishments worked with a series of buttonhole stitches.

A total of no more than thirty bobbins were required for making free lace, and this perhaps was another reason for its popularity. This work was so much easier to handle than other types, some of which required the use of a great many more threads at one time. The round pillow generally used no more than thirty bobbins although lace could be made on it with less. A square pillow could use as many as 100 bobbins. The more bobbins used and the more intertwining of thread, the more involved the pattern would naturally become. Free laces, incidentally, have never been satisfactorily duplicated by machine, mostly because of the intricacy of the various designs involved.

Oblong, oval, and mushroom-shaped as well as bolster and cylindrical pillows were also frequently used in the making of bobbin lace. All pillows, of whatever shape, were usually filled as hard as possible with chopped hay, straw, chaff, horsehair, or other similar material. There were often slight variations from the standard sizes of the pillows too, these depending on the needs of the individual worker for his comfort and on what might be most suitable for the particular project being worked on.

Lace made on other than a round pillow was known as straight lace—*fils continué*—and many of the pieces made in this way, such as the Cluny and Mechlin laces, were very easily copied by machine. In the making of the straight laces, however, both the motif and the fond were often done simultaneously, and the fond was worked in various ways, each different way becoming an integral part of a particular design. To the collector, the type of fond used is an important criterion for the authenticity of a given piece of work. A hexagonal fond, for example, was the type used for the making of all Valenciennes lace, a variety that was made with all the threads put on the pillow at one time. The design was formed by repeating a single pattern over and over again. As a rule, most straight lace pieces were made in this way, and the pattern was generally a small all-over repeat, the work at times involving as many as a hundred bobbins in use at one time, with all the threads being pinned to the top of the lace-making pillow.

With the coming of the Machine Age early in the nineteenth century, at about the time of the peak of both the needlepoint and bobbin lace-making industries in Europe, machinery was invented with which one could easily duplicate many of the different kinds of mesh backgrounds used for the various laces. A complete new style of lace-making was developed, and many designs could now be worked by hand over the machine-made nets. Lace made in this way became known as *needlerun* lace, and much of this type of work was very fine and bore a very direct resemblance to the pieces that until then had been made entirely by hand.

Needlerun laces became very popular in the many countries to which the lace-making industry had spread. Some of the loveliest examples are the Spanish Blonde laces and the lovely Limerick and Carrickmacross pieces from Ireland. It is not at all difficult to understand how and why needlerun laces were soon substituted for the wonderful true laces, since with this new method it was far simpler to work designs that were quite comparable in beauty to many of the earlier pieces. Needlerun lace involved only the tracing of a design onto a piece of white glazed material on which spaces had been left for filling, and then smoothly stretching the manufactured net over the material, and basting it into place. The pattern was then completed by hand, working with a needle onto the net, following the traced design and then working any of a great variety of fillings into the free spaces formed between the designs. These fillings were usually made with the aid of an embroidery hoop used to hold the working surface smooth and taut.

While many of the needlerun laces were

Fichu, needlerun pattern on machine-made net. Irish, Limerick, early nineteenth century. Victoria and Albert Museum, London (Crown Copyright)

rather close duplications of the pieces that had formerly been made entirely by hand, one particular variety of this type of work was a little unusual, and perhaps stands in a class of its own. This was the very beautiful Carrickmacross lace, made on machine-made net grounds but also very often made *guipure,*

Shawl, appliqué bobbin lace on machine-made net. Brussels, mid-nineteenth century. Victoria and Albert Museum, London (Crown Copyright)

Collar, applied laces. Irish, Carrickmacross. Late nineteenth century. The Metropolitan Museum of Art, New York (Gift of David Dows, 1952)

which means that there was an open space treatment behind the design, rather than a firm background of any kind. When Carrickmacross was worked on net in the more usual needlerun manner, the net was placed between the muslin and the tracing, and the work was then done through both of these surfaces. Spaces were usually planned in the original design for the use of interesting fillings, to be darned onto the net in the same way as they were worked on other needlerun designs.

When Carrickmacross was made *guipure*, however, it had the special characteristic of being a very attractive and unusual kind of lace, no matter how simple the lines might be, nor how enlarged the patterns. When the work was done this way, the design was traced on white glazed material, with fine muslin on top and a layer of unbleached muslin underneath to provide more ease in working. All pieces were basted smoothly and firmly together, and the work was done on the muslin by running a strong thread or cord along the outline and then whipping fine stitches over it. Those spaces that had been designed to be open in the pattern were then connected with *Venetian bars*, which were made by working a series of close buttonhole stitches over any given group of several threads. When the design was completed, the fine muslin was very carefully removed from the tracing, and the ground of unbleached muslin under the open spaces was cut away. The clipping had to be close enough to the cord

so that the work looked neat, yet not close enough to damage it.

Part II of this book will tell you of many additional methods of making lace. Most of these laces are often referred to as the "implement" laces, since they involve some kind of an implement or tool to work with. The group includes those crafts which are a source of great pleasure to people who enjoy creating their own things today. Knitting, crocheting, tatting, and hairpin lace techniques are shown, some of them new, and some dating far back to antiquity, to the time when man first realized that with a strand of yarn and some simple tool he could fashion interesting and very functional articles of clothing for himself. A shuttle is used for tatting, a loom or fork for hairpin lace, and a crochet hook or a pair of knitting needles for the crocheted or knitted laces.

While none of these laces is considered to be comparable in fineness or value to the laces thus far described, they are nevertheless quite lovely, and do have a particular merit of their own. The ease with which they can be worked and the sturdier materials which can be used in their making place them in the category of lovely "products of our times," laces that we can enjoy making and using. And, since they do have this merit, that portion of the book offers several contemporary designs made in the various media, and directions so that a lace-maker of today will be able to make them for her own pleasure and personal use.

TWO

Many Loved Lace in Many Ways

There is little doubt that the discovery of lace introduced to the world a beautiful commodity that has been a source of pleasure and delight ever since. Early man loved the addition of the decorative finery to his rather drab clothing. The church felt that the white, airy purity of lace was especially fitting and symbolic of the beauty and spirit of God. Members of the Renaissance nobility vied with each other for possession of it and new ways to adorn themselves with it, and even Napoleon, the fearsome warrior, loved it to a passion and went to very great extremes to buy it for his own personal use and for the pleasure of those around him.

It is not a simple matter to determine whose particular love and admiration for lace did the most to foster its universal popularity. We already know of man's preoccupation with it very many centuries ago, and how the

art of lace-making spread from the Middle East onto the mainland of Europe where it developed to magnificent beauty and perfection. We have learned of the appeal of the rather ethereal texture and look of lace to members of the clergy, who early in time valued the use of fine lace even above their beautiful damasks and embroidered silks. Evidence of this interest is a famous lace alb stored among the prized art treasures in the Sistine Chapel at the Vatican. This alb is supposed to have been worn by Pope Boniface VIII in 1298, and it is thought that it was brought to Rome by St. Nilor and his monks when they were driven east by the Saracens in the tenth century. In the archives of the Catholic church there are many fine examples of beautiful old drawnwork and cutwork altar pieces and vestments and some pieces combining these two kinds of lace with reticello,

Early Papal costume. Munchener Bilderbogen, Munich

the very early type which dates back practically as far as the history of lace-making itself. Many of the pieces have very elaborately patterned designs including, amid flowers and leaves, signs of the cross and of the pomegranate, a symbol often used in textiles made for the clergy.

Much of the lace used by the church was made by the nuns in the convents who practiced lace-making, along with other arts, as a service to the church. Many more of the finer pieces, however, including altar cloths, magnificent white surplices worn over the robes of many bishops, cardinals, and other members of the officiating hierarchy of the church, and many smaller pieces such as those used to cover the communion vessels, were presented to the church as gifts by the nobility, who had hoped with the presentation of these gifts to gain political favor from the powers of the church. Many of the finest lace workers had been commissioned to make these pieces, and it is interesting to note that a great number of the old ecclesiastical pieces have been preserved because they were carefully put away in vaults at various times when too lavish a display of finery was considered to be in poor taste, even for the men of God. One such time was when the devout King Louis XIII of France issued strong edicts against the extravagant use of lace in dress of any kind. Another such period was at the time of the rise of Protestantism when members of the Catholic church felt that it was necessary to put a curb on their former self-indulgences and to salvage their holy image by living more frugally and limiting their use of lace and other fine treasures.

In telling of the love of the church for fine lace, we should in no way neglect the interest shown by the nuns, who have always been very preoccupied with the study and practice of lace-making. Aside from the work which they did as a service for the church, they were inspired by the beauty of lace and intrigued by the various methods of making it. Dedicated to be of service to the poor, they set up many convent schools and, throughout the centuries, busied themselves with teaching the art to those who were in need and to all who wanted to learn. Although it is true that the work done in the convents was not particularly innovative in the creation of designs, it is also true that the quiet patience and very disciplined skill of the sisters contributed a great deal to the advancement of the art, and was indeed responsible for much of the very fine work that was done throughout the world.

In discussing the very delicate art of lace-making, it is impossible not to become involved with the history, both passive and violent, of the world itself. The growth of the lace-making industry in Flanders and in Italy during the fifteenth and sixteenth centuries has already been discussed. But we must talk now of one Italian noblewoman who loved lace above all other material possessions and who, almost single-handedly, played a very major role in the progress of the art.

Catherine de Medici, who lived from 1519 to 1589, was strong of mind and strong of heart and was fascinated by the beauty of lace. Early an avid collector of fine pieces, she gathered together and kept within her household the finest lace workers from all over Italy. As a member of the great and noble Medici family whose interests lay in the advancement of all of the arts, she had her group of prized workers teach the lace-making skill to many other people. She herself accumulated lace for her own personal use to such a point that her zealousness in this

Ecclesiastical costume. Punto in aria and linen alb. Italian, early seventeenth century. The Metropolitan Museum of Art, New York (Bequest of Mable M. Fahnestock, 1931)

direction might be compared somewhat to that of the legendary old man who liked pancakes so much that he accumulated and saved whole trunkfuls of them. At one time an inventory of Catherine's property showed her to be in possession of one coffer containing 381 exquisite lace squares and of another containing 538.

Catherine de Medici, wearing a linen upturned collar of cutwork and needlepoint lace. Early sixteenth century. The Louvre

"Isabel of France" by Pourbus. Costume, sixteenth century, Flemish. By permission of Messrs. Braun, Clement & Co., Dornach (Alsace) and Paris

Aside from her own personal preoccupation with this beautiful finery, however, Catherine's great influence in the cultivation of the art took form when she married King Henry II of France and brought with her to that country her enthusiasm, her coffers full of beautiful lace, and her skilled workers.

Until then, the French had been content to import the lace they used, but inspired by Catherine's enthusiasm and her beautiful collection, they quickly learned to make their own. Thus they were started on the path that

was to lead them in a very short time to the establishment of one of the greatest lace-making centers in the world. Suddenly, they wanted possession of all the lace they could have. They took full advantage of the knowledge of their Queen's strongly disciplined lace workers, and they learned to copy many of the beautiful designs that she had brought with her from Italy.

Almost immediately the French created new fashion trends involving the use of lace, and as they became more busied with this preoccupation, they found themselves running into, among other problems, the difficulty of being able to get enough new patterns to satisfy their needs and to maintain themselves, both individually and collectively, as the new lace fashion pace-setters of the world. An enterprising publisher of Cologne, a Pierre Quinty, attempted to solve this problem, and fairly early in the sixteenth century came out with what was probably the very first needlework book ever published. The book bore, in translation, the staggering title of "A New and Subtle Book Concerning the Art and Science of Embroidery, Fringes, Tapestry-Making, as Well as That of Other Crafts Done With the Needle." It offered many new patterns and, an instant and tremendous success, it went through many editions and was translated into various languages, including German, where the author was referred to as *Quintell*. Significantly, this book did much to foster the making and wearing of lace and was followed by the publication of many other books of this type.

One book of particular interest was written later in the century by Frederic Vinciolo, a gentleman who had been brought to France as lace-maker to the court by Catherine de Medici. His book, after a flowery dedication to the Queen, proclaimed, "I have greatly desired, honorable readers, to place before you for works of a magnificent standard the present designs which I have kept back, hidden and unknown, until now when I offer them with a cheerful heart to the French nation."

Scholars' scrutiny of the book has since revealed that much of it was neither hidden nor unknown, but rather pirated directly from other lace-makers.

As more books followed, however, more designs were revealed, and as patterns became more elaborate and beautiful, the craze for fashions using lace became ever more exaggerated and grandiose. Lovers of lace, particularly among the French, soared to ridiculous heights in their use of it. The comparatively simple pleated and fluted collars, known as *ruffs*, a style which had originated in Italy, became very popular in France, and before very long the French lords and ladies had magnified the style to the point where they vied to outdo each other with bigger and more elaborate ruffs. Writers of the times quickly made them the butt of their jokes, and one in particular described one of the more elaborate collars as being "gadrooned like organ pipes, contorted and crinkled like cabbage, and big as the sails of a windmill." Certainly worse, however, than the doubtful embarrassment that might have been caused by this ridicule was the torture and discomfort suffered by some of those who chose to indulge in such high fashion. Many of the very huge pieces needed to be supported with hoops of iron or wire. Perhaps one of the most ridiculous instances of suffering for a cause is that of one noble lady, Renée Margot, who preferred to eat her soup with a specially made spoon having a handle two feet long rather than remove her ruff at the dining table.

Rembrandt's "Portrait of a Woman." Dutch, early sixteenth century. The Metropolitan Museum of Art, New York (Bequest of Mrs. H. O. Havemeyer, 1929. The H. O. Havemeyer Collection)

Although some lace styles were so very elaborate and extreme, there were other lace fashions which were also loved and widely used, but in a more sensible way and by those of lesser means who could not possibly afford the extravagances of the aristocracy. The barber, the sculptor, and even the warrior chose to wear lace just as much as their titled contemporaries did. There were dresses and caps for babies, too, and collars and cuffs for the ladies, and lovely though very simple trimmings and edgings for their hats and gloves.

Although these were indeed to be counted among the important fashions of the day, too, it is perhaps because of their simplicity that one does not hear too much of them. For that reason the role they played in the history of lace-making was not nearly as important as that of the more frivolous styles which catered to the indulgences of the upper classes.

Catherine's son, Henry III, inherited his mother's taste in many areas, particularly her great love and passion for lace. He had such a reverence for it that he refused to allow his servants, or even his courtiers, to handle his precious ruffs, but chose rather to carefully wash and iron them himself!

His son and successor, Henry IV, who reigned from 1553 to 1610, was also obsessed with his family's passion for lace. It was during his reign that the use of it in dress soared to new and unheard-of extremes, notably among men. They used it, not only as great collars and cuffs on their doublets, but also as trim on their breeches and boot tops. When they did not wear boots, they used lace on their shoes, which were adorned with elaborate rosettes made of either lace or ribbon, and on their garters, which were long sashes tied under the knee with a big bow, the ends edged with lace and sometimes hanging halfway down the calves of their legs.

Such costumes were often depicted in many important seventeenth-century fashion engravings and etchings, notably those of Abraham Bosse, Jacques Callot, Bernard Picart, and Jean Dieu de St. Jean. The time finally came, however, when even Henry IV himself became a little annoyed with these overindulgences, although he did attempt to rationalize that perhaps this type of extravagance was a good way of promoting the lace-making industry of France. His First Minister, however, took a more pessimistic view of all that was going on, and he feared financial ruin to many of the noblemen because of their ridiculous expenditures in the cause of vanity. The King was strongly reprimanded for allowing this nonsense to go on. "You need and want iron and soldiers, not lace and silks to trick out our fops!" As a result of the minister's attitude, several edicts were issued limiting the use of lace in dress. The edicts, however, were rather mild in content and little effort was made to enforce them. Henry's heart was not really in it, and the craze, of course, continued.

The history of lace-making in seventeenth-century France is fascinating indeed, and it is interesting to note how much it was influenced by the individual personalities of the rulers of the period. The austere and rigidly religious King Louis XIII, who succeeded the gentle, more pleasure-loving Henry IV, was so moved by such frivolity as that of one courtier of the time who boasted that he wore thirty-two acres of his best vineyard around his neck (referring to the sale of his prime land to purchase the ruff he was wearing), that he issued a strong edict on "The Regulation of Superfluity in Costume," restricting the use of lace in dress for both men and

Morcelse's portrait of Amelie Elisabeth, Comtesse de Hainault, wearing a ruff of reticello. Early seventeenth century. The Hague. By permission of Messrs. Braun, Clement & Co., Dornach (Alsace) and Paris

women to the barest minimum. Although this edict was extremely distasteful to many, it was enforced for a while, in spite of the added burden of ridicule of many of the artists of the time. Abraham Bosse, in particular, boldly caricatured men and women as dressed in the ultimate extreme of ridiculously plain clothes, sadly eyeing the lace-laden finery that they could no longer wear.

With the accession of King Louis XIV to the throne, however, all of the sober efforts of his predecessor were thrown to the wind.

Many Loved Lace in Many Ways   33

"Habit Noir." Engraving by Jean Dieu de St. Jean the elder.
French, mid-seventeenth century

The new King ushered in the most glorious period of lace-making in France or, as some contend, lace-making anywhere in the world. Besides his own love and lavish personal use of it, which he commanded to be emulated by his court, he envisioned the possibilities of creating a great lace-making industry in France, and he made, with the cooperation and shrewd guidance of his Minister of Finance, Jean Baptiste de Colbert, a strong and deliberate effort to replace Italy as the great lace-making center of the world. Young French girls were sent to Venice to learn the art, and some of the best lace workers were lured from Venice to France. Lace-making centers were set up in various parts of the country, most notably at Alençon and Argentan. Since Venetian law forbade the making of their beautiful point de Venise outside of their country, the French copy was called point de France, and the Italian gros point de Venise, which was also copied, became known as point Colbert.

Venetian authorities, however, were not about to accept the French competition lightly. Extremely resentful when the full impact of the growing rivalry reached them, they did everything in their power to maintain their own prime position in the lace-making world. Typical of the manner in which they tried to control the situation was one Venetian decree which read, in effect: "If any artist or handcraftsman practices his art in any foreign land to the detriment of the Republic, orders for his return will be sent to him; if he disobeys them, his nearest of kin will be put into prison in order that through his interest in their welfare, his obedience may be compelled. If he comes back, his past offense will be condoned and employment for him will be found in Venice, but if notwithstanding the imprisonment of his nearest kin he obstinately decides to continue living abroad, an emmissary will be commissioned to kill him, and his next of kin will be liberated only upon his death."

Though this harsh edict did frighten a few workers into returning to Venice, actually it came too late to affect the rapidly growing industry in France, where lace centers had sprung up all over. Many new and distinctive patterns were developed, some indeed far more delicate and superior to those that were being made in Italy. Many of today's experts regard the laces produced in France during this period as the finest in the world, although there are others who prefer the rich flowing design and the heavier corded treatment of the Venetian laces to the sharp, crisp, and finely detailed French designs. Be this as it may, at one point during Colbert's great effort to establish his country as the greatest lace-making center of the world, he remarked, "Fashion is to France what the gold of Peru is to Spain." If the French could not satisfy their great desire for lace fashions at home they could go elsewhere, but he personally intended to keep the industry in France and to use the French skill and design sense to develop their own style and to promote it to the rest of the world. In this he succeeded admirably.

Abraham Bosse's engraving illustrating plainer style of dress adapted after edicts were issued against extravagance. French, mid-seventeenth century

King Louis XIV of France

Jean Baptiste Colbert

It is difficult in relating a tale about lace not to go on endlessly with stories of the many very fascinating events of history that affected and were affected by the practice of the art. The great French lace-making industry suffered a most disastrous blow in 1685 with the revocation of the Edict of Nantes, which caused skilled lace workers, among many others, to leave the country in droves, seeking religious tolerance elsewhere. An even harsher blow was the advent of the French Revolution, which put lace in a position of great disfavor because it was a symbol of the hated ruling class. Yet the person who was responsible for reviving it and restoring it once more to its peak was the ruthless warrior, Napoleon Bonaparte.

It is indeed a strange twist of character that this strong and fearsome ruler could possibly cherish anything as fine and delicate as lace, yet it was the most gossamer of pieces which seemed to appeal to him most. In addition to Napoleon's maneuvering of everything within his power and strength to redevelop the lace-making industry as an important means of bringing wealth and prosperity back to France, he personally purchased and indulged in the use of laces which were surely to be counted among the most costly and extravagant pieces ever made.

His magnificent *equipage de lit*, or bed furnishings, were the most perfect and most valuable point d'Alençon pieces ever made. This masterpiece, commanded as a gift for the Empress Josephine, was so great an undertaking that it unfortunately could not be completed before his matrimonial arrangements needed to be reconsidered in the light of political developments, and it was used as his wedding gift to Marie Louise, Archduchess of Austria, at the time of his marriage to her. This *equipage de lit* consisted of two curtains, each measuring 144 inches wide and 98 inches high, valances that measured 279 inches by 19 inches, a 75 by 80-inch bedspread, and a 45-inch square canopy. Though the dimensions of this set were so very great,

"Concert at Versailles," early seventeenth century

the work was filled with intricate detail, and each part of the whole was comparable in workmanship to the finest masterpiece ever worked in this delicate art. Many tiny bees, Napoleon's symbol, adorn the set, and the Napoleonic crown appears in the corner sections. The pieces, made in a deep cream color, are bordered with lilies, the exotic flowers with which Josephine had filled the garden at Malmaison.

This work of art is said to have cost 40,000 francs at the time it was made. Many parts of it can be found in various museums throughout the world, most of them in excellent condition, except for a sinister stain in one corner of the bedspread which is reported to have been caused by the blood of a soldier who fought to save the lace when it was being carried away from France at the time of Napoleon's downfall.

Many Loved Lace in Many Ways   **39**

Madame Louis de France, seventeenth century

Costume of striped taffeta with silver lace, said to have been made by Mme. Bertin, dressmaker to Marie Antoinette. French, late eighteenth century. The Metropolitan Museum of Art, New York (Rogers Fund, 1932)

Other countries besides France and Italy also showed a great admiration for the delicate finery of lace and in some instances they too were quite carried away with their desire to possess and display it. Certainly not to be overlooked in any account of those who loved lace very much is King Charles I of England, who reigned in the mid-seventeenth century and is known to have carefully noted that he had bought 1,600 yards of magnificent lace trimming—1,000 yards for one dozen day shirts and 600 yards for night shirts. Another lover of lace was Archduke Albert of Austria who was portrayed in an early seventeenth-century Johannes Muller engraving as wearing a "grand collar," or ruff, which was so enormous that it practically severed his head from the rest of his body.

King Philip IV of Spain was so preoccupied with the fashion of lace collars that one of the important edicts of his reign decreed that the *golilla*, a heavily starched lace collar resting on wired "underproppers," must replace any other kind of lace neckwear being worn at the time. One of the sadder tales is the total loss to posterity of King Henry VIII's many yards of gold edging for his shirts. None has been preserved, most of it having been thrown at one time or another into the various melting pots of rebellious people interested only in the value of the melted metal.

If the story of the fashionable use of lace has seemed to concentrate to this point rather strongly on the male interest in lace, it is because today such masculine usage seems a bit unusual. The structural delicacy, fineness, and lightness of this type of material would tend to make one rather associate it with the distaff side. Certainly women, too, have admired and loved it very much. Catherine de Medici was not alone in her great love for lace, nor even in her influence in spreading this love among others.

Queen Elizabeth of England was much like Catherine in that she used as much lace as she could for her own personal dress and also did a great deal to advance the various lace fashions in her own kingdom. A particular fondness of hers was for the large flat collars which were made of Dutch linen, beautifully garnished with lace and worn perked up fan-wise at the back of women's heads. Conscious of her own lack of beauty, Elizabeth had tried always to make up for it with rather elaborate dress, and it was because of this that lace suited her taste so perfectly well. Cherishing expensive and elaborate gowns as she did, at the time of her death

Point d'Alençon bed curtains from Napoleon's *garniture de lit.* Brooks Memorial Art Gallery, Memphis (Gift of Warner S. McCall as a memorial to Jennie Owen McCall)

Leon Alphonse Noel's "Portrait of the Empress Eugenie." French, mid-nineteenth century. The Metropolitan Museum of Art, New York (Harris Brisbane Dick Fund, 1932)

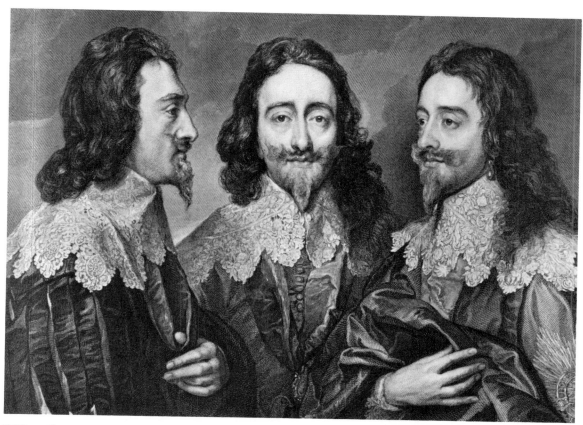

William Sharp's engraving of Sir Anthony van Dyck's portrait of Charles I of England. Cooper-Hewitt Museum of Decorative Arts and Design, Smithsonian Institution, New York (Ex coll. Mr. and Mrs. William Franklin Mitchell)

she owned more than 1,000 gowns, most of them embellished with lace, and many of them with gold and silver lace imported from Genoa, some pieces even trimmed with inserts of precious jewels. Chapter 3, "Lace-Making Around the World," will tell more about the strong influence Elizabeth had on her countrymen who, emulating and copying her style, learned to make lovely lace of their own. It was during her reign that English Honiton lace became popular. It was named after the town which became one of the world's fairly important lace-making centers.

Queen Victoria too, though far simpler of taste than Elizabeth, loved lace and wore it rather freely, but more as a means of encouraging the English lace industry than for personal reasons. At her marriage when she was only 18, she chose a veil and gown of English Honiton rather than any other that she might have had made of a choice of very fine imported lace. This she did to please her coun-

Anthony van Dyck's "Robert Rich, Earl of Warwick." The Metropolitan Museum of
Art, New York (The Jules S. Bache Collection, 1949)

trymen and to stimulate their interest in their own product. Later she made a point of wearing lace in her daily dress, also to encourage the style among the women in her kingdom, and to help at the same time the people of Ireland who were suffering a famine and had just been taught the art of lace-making as a possible means of being able to alleviate their woes. Victoria was most always seen wearing a lace shawl, and after she was widowed, she usually completed her dress with a touch of black lace.

Many have loved lace, each in his or her own way, and for his own reason. Some have cherished it purely for personal adornment, others have respected it as a symbol of wealth, and still others have used it for political reasons and as a means of promoting industry for their countries. In a little different, but surely a charming way, even the home-loving Dutch had a great admiration for lace, and they were the only ones who chose to use it especially for the decoration of their treasured household objects. They put lace bows on the handles of their polished tankards and braziers, for example. Another rather unusual custom of theirs was to tie lace around the doorknocker of their home to announce the birth of a child; this served the practical purpose at the same time of muffling the sound of the knocker so that the new baby would not wake up when callers came to visit.

To those with some familiarity with lace-making, the name of Barbara Uttmann is certainly not unfamiliar. She was another one who loved lace in a quite different way and who, like Catherine de Medici, played a historic role in the history of the art, her influence being in the area of bobbin lace, in contrast to Catherine's which was in the area of fine needlepoint lace.

Barbara Uttmann had learned the art of bobbin lace-making from Brabant refugees who had settled in her native Nuremberg, in Germany. When she married, she moved to Annaberg where along with her husband, Christopher, she practiced and became highly skilled in the then little-known art of lace-making. Being of simple taste herself, Barbara Uttmann's main interest in bobbin lace-making was to teach it to others, rather than to use it for personal adornment. Toward this end she started a school in her home, and her lace-making was so beautiful and her teaching methods so successful that young girls who began training with her at the age of 5 had become expert enough to earn their own living by the time they were 13.

Other schools using her teaching methods were soon established throughout the country, and pillow or bobbin lace-making became quite an active occupation in Germany. By 1561 the efforts of this great person had organized an industry that employed some 30,000 persons in the manufacture of lace. Her fame spread to other parts of the world.

To conclude this chapter about the love of so many people for lace, we would like to tell just one more little story, in part a fantasy this time, but indeed a very charming one.

Albert, Archduke of Austria

Royal costume, mid-seventeenth century

Frans Hals' "Claes Duyst van Voorhout." The Metropolitan Museum of Art, New York (The Jules S. Bache Collection, 1949)

Orsetta. The young couple pledged their eternal love for one another, but unfortunately soon after this Martino had to sail away again, and Orsetta began her long wait for his return. As the tale goes, it was during this long voyage that Martino, his heart so full of love, heard for the first time the voice of the mermaids, who were known by legend to bewitch men with their lovely mortal singing. It was believed that no man had ever been able to resist the mysterious beckoning of these sea creatures, and that those who ventured into the waves to follow them were always destined to perish.

Martino's sailmates, aware of the omen and frightened by the sound of the beautiful voices, bound themselves with rope to the mast of their ship to protect themselves. Only Martino refused to do so. "I will resist," he said to his companions. "My love for Orsetta is far stronger than any rope." While the others remained bound, yet craved to follow the mermaids, Martino listened calmly to the fatal enchanted singing. Aware at once that someone was resisting their fascination, the mermaids became angry and went to confer with their queen. "Your Majesty," one said, "there is a young man, unbound, who remains indifferent to our charm." The proud queen rose immediately from her coral throne and came up rapidly to the surface of the sea. Leaning against the railing of the galleon, she said, "Martino, what spell has made you remain insensible to our enchantment?"

"No spell, queen," he replied calmly, "it

If we were to title the story, we would call it "The Lace of the Mermaids." The setting is in Burano, a tiny secluded island in the Mediterranean, not very far from Venice, and famous for its lace-making industry which existed during the eighteenth and nineteenth centuries, and which is flourishing again as a source of income for its people.

The fantasy part of the story starts with the return of Martino, a young sailor just home from sailing the seven seas, and suddenly in love with the beautiful young maiden,

48   The Story of Lace

Queen Elizabeth I of England

Barbara Uttmann

Burano bridal veil in the "Spirit of the Gift of the Mermaids." Ditto Jesurum (Lace Specialists), Venice (By permission of Compagnia Italiana Dei Grandi Alberghi)

is my love for a young woman which gives me strength to resist your enticing call."

The queen then disappeared back into the waves, and after a short while returned with a swarm of young maidens who, at her command, began to flip their fins until the sea bubbled with foam. In another instant, the foam solidified.

"Take it, Martino," said the queen, placing at his feet a very light cloak of foam. "This is our wedding gift to Orsetta."

Lace-making in Burano today. Ditto Jesurum, Venice (By permission of Compagnia Italiana Dei Grandi Alberghi)

When Martino returned home, the marriage of the couple was celebrated, and Orsetta approached the altar wrapped in her beautiful lace veil. Having never seen such a spectacular vision before, the women of the island worked day and night in a great effort to try to make another such piece. Spreading it on a table, they studied it intently and with needle and thread in hand, they tried to imitate the tiny roses, the airy scallops, and the myriad of drops that the sea foam, solidi-fying, had whimsically created. Stitch upon stitch, knot upon knot, and with patient and nimble fingers, they did finally copy the mermaids' miracle and did re-create the lace whose beauty was born of the foam of the sea.

The women are still making lace in Burano today. The pattern design of Orsetta's bridal veil remains a thing of beauty forever, and the Burano ladies remain among the very few inspired fine lace-makers today.

Many Loved Lace in Many Ways **51**

THREE

Lace-Making Around the World

The growth of the lace-making industry around the world is one of the rather fascinating aspects of the art. It has created innumerable patterns and designs that are unique and distinctive, each representing quite clearly the area in which the lace was made. Lace-making is a true art form, and like other creative work, it most naturally reflects the taste, the feeling, and the individual personality characteristics of those who were involved with it. It has also always been influenced by the environment in which it was practiced: such practical considerations as the availability of thread in a particular area, the expertise of the teachers there, the organization of the workers, and the actual use for the product itself in terms of, for instance, whether the demand for the finished work was for local use or export.

An example in point would be the fact that,

for natural reasons, the lace-making industry was never a flourishing one in parts of the Orient. Known there from earliest times, perhaps even before its appearance in the Middle East, it was never practiced on any large scale, presumably because, for instance, the climate in China is ideal for the raising of mulberry trees and silkworms, and although many fine laces have been made of silk, the Chinese preferred to use their raw product for the manufacture of heavy silk and brocade materials. Since these fabrics were certainly more suitably adorned with their own exquisite silk embroidery than with lace, which was of much too delicate a texture, it is obvious that there never was any strong motivation for the lace industry to have flourished there.

There is a great deal to tell, however, about the lace-making endeavors in those parts of the world where it did flourish, and as we wander together to these different places, it is perhaps best to learn of the development of the art in the order of the progress of time, and to include as we go many of the interesting little sidelights as to how and why each did become important.

We have already discussed the prime position of Venice as the great center of needlepoint lace-making in very early times and its headstart advantage having been its proximity to the sea and its accessibility to news from the Middle East where, presumably, lace making had its earliest start. Evidence of this foreign influence can be seen in the translation of the arabesques of Persian rug designs and tooled leather work, combined with the floral motifs of Rhodian pottery, all beautifully translated by the Venetians into very fine needlepoint patterns.

That the art of lace-making reached unsur-passed heights in Venice during the Middle Ages and shortly thereafter is best seen by the achievement of such magnificent pieces as the entire group of point de Venise laces, including the gros point de Venise, plat point de Venise, point de Venise à rose (Venetian rose point), and the punto Rosaline, known sometimes as point de neige. All these laces were indeed beautiful and certainly related to each other, although each had its own very special characteristics.

Gros point de Venise is noted for its continuous scrolls of floral and foliated forms, joined together with a series of brides. The forms themselves were heavily outlined with cordonnet, which was worked with a thicker thread or a series of buttonhole stitches superimposed one over the other, thus lending almost a three-dimensional sculptural quality to the lace.

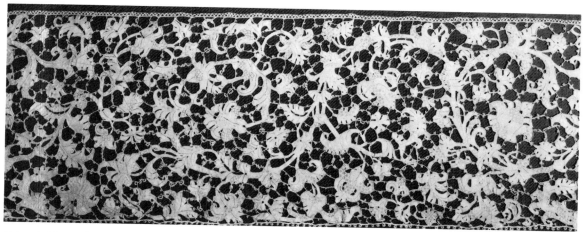

Point de Venise lace flounce. Italian, early seventeenth century. Corcoran Gallery of Art, Washington, D.C.

Lace-Making Around the World **53**

Point de Venise altar frontal. Italian, eighteenth century. Corcoran Gallery of Art, Washington, D.C.

This type of work gave way later to the lighter and flatter designs of the point plat de Venise pieces, in which the heavier treatment was eliminated and more dainty patterns were used, predominantly those which added a type of branching quality to the appearance of the work. With the Venetian rose point, however, we encounter again all the characteristics of the cordonnet treatment of the gros point de Venise, but with the patterns worked on a much smaller and finer scale. The style here still follows the serpentine, scroll-like designs of the earlier gros point de Venise, but loses much of its strength through the use of many picots and small flowerlike clusters of stitches embroidered over the brides, thus giving a generally softer look to the work.

There is no doubt that one of the heights of Venetian lace craftsmanship was reached with the punto Rosaline, where the scroll pattern disappeared completely, leaving just minute branching and intervening bars. What was at first only a connecting bar in the gros point de Venise pieces grew to be an integral part of the pattern itself, often referred to as the "candlestick" pattern and beautifully enhanced with picots, flowerlike clusters and cordonnet.

Related, finally, to the Venetian point family and considered to be the epitome of all the Venetian work, was the point de Venise à réseau, the most delicate of all the needle-point fabrics, examples of which are, unfortunately, practically nonexistent. Those few which can be found are highly prized by collectors of fine pieces. The designs of this lace

Gros point de Venise border. Late seventeenth century. Victoria and Albert Museum, London (Crown Copyright)

Plat point de Venise à réseau lappet. Early eighteenth century. Victoria and Albert Museum, London (Crown Copyright)

are very similar to the leaf and flower motifs appearing in gros point de Venise, but the lace is embedded in a réseau, or net. The pattern is not outlined with cordonnet, and it is no longer held together by brides placed at random, the connecting device in this lace being an overall mesh. Point de Venise à réseau seems to have marked a final growth stage in the making of fine Venetian laces and from this point on the desire for light and delicate pieces challenged Venetian lace-makers to designs made on finer and thinner réseaux, until they finally achieved pieces that were almost spiderweblike in appearance.

Lace-Making Around the World   **55**

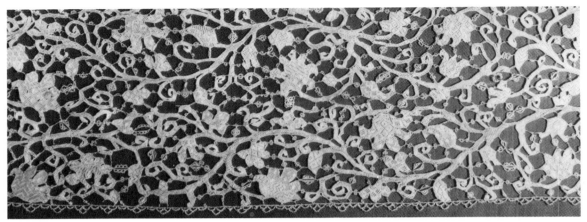

Plat point de Venise border. Italian, eighteenth century. Corcoran Gallery of Art, Washington, D.C. (W. A. Clark Collection)

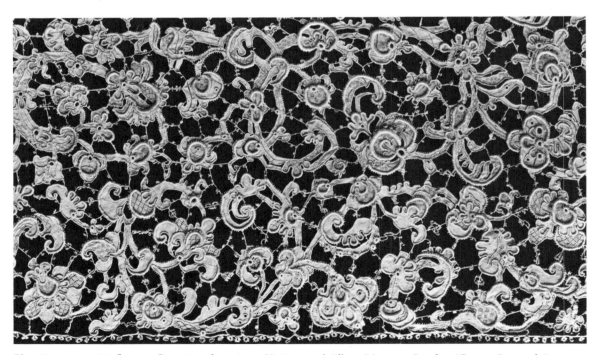

Venetian rose point flounce. Seventeenth century. Victoria and Albert Museum, London (Crown Copyright)

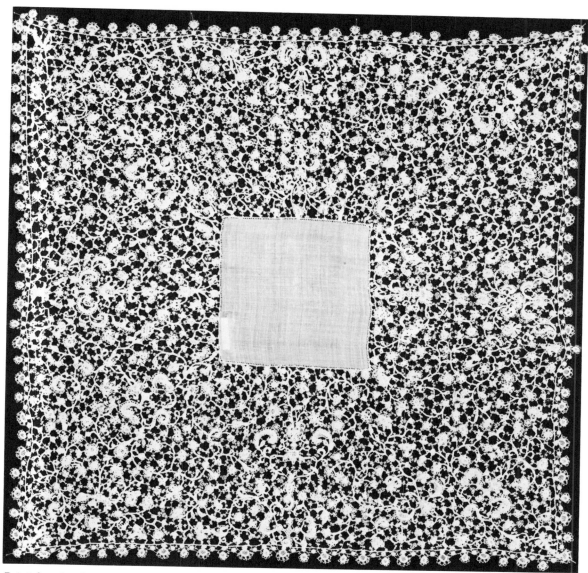

Point de neige deep edging. Italian, late seventeenth century.(Victoria and Albert Museum, London
(Crown Copyright)

Rosaline point/pearl de Venise flounce. Italian. Corcoran Gallery of Art, Washington, D.C.
(In the W. A. Clark Collection)

Point de Venise à réseau cap crown. Italian, early
eighteenth century. Cooper-Hewitt Museum of
Decorative Arts and Design, Smithsonian Institution,
New York

Though handmade Venetian laces are truly
magnificent and considered to be among the
finest in the world, it is nevertheless a little
sad that the great achievement of this lace-
making center tended to overshadow some of
the other very interesting work that was being
done in other parts of Italy. The cities of
Genoa and Milan certainly were important
lace-making centers.

Genoa, in particular, was famed for its lace
made of gold and silver thread, a rather unusual type of work indigenous to that particular city because of its closeness to Cyprus

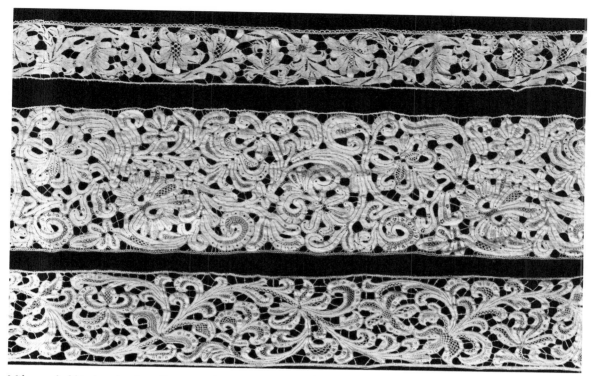

Milanese bobbin lace borders. Seventeenth century. Victoria and Albert Museum, London (Crown Copyright)

from where one could import quantities of the metal threads. These beautiful laces became so important as a Genoese export product for royalty of other countries that citizens of the area were strictly forbidden to use any for themselves. The typical free expression of the Italian personality, already evidenced in the work that had been done in Venice, was further reflected in the styling of many of the Genoese and Milanese designs. Lace-makers of Genoa often mixed both bobbin and needlepoint pieces at will, much as it suited their fancy and taste; and those in Milan created many interesting laces too, one particular one which was made of purple silk, ornamented in gold. This lace, incidentally, was said to have been cherished by, among others, King Henry VIII of England, who used it as an important part of many of his regal costumes.

The peasant laces of Italy also show a great deal of artistic quality and many have a distinctive beauty of their own, coarse as they may be, but excitingly free in expression. *Punto Avorio*, which was made in Valle Vogna, a district of Northern Italy, was an

Panel of bobbin lace à brides. Milanese, seventeenth century. Victoria and Albert Museum, London
(Crown Copyright)

unusual type of Italian peasant lace, and involved closely worked needlepoint bands of silk and linen. *Point d'Argentelle*, a lace made not far from Genoa, appears to have fairly well copied and embellished upon the point d'Alençon designs that were made in France. Besides adding its own variation of design to the light delicateness of those patterns, this particular lace has a special distinctive quality due to the unusual whiteness of its threads.

Among the most unusual and distinctive of the Italian peasant laces are those which were and are still being made in Burano, the tiny island off the coast of Venice, where one of the few lace-making centers in the world today still exists. Burano lace, the "origin" of which was related at the end of Chapter 2, is usually identified by the vertically worked mesh of unevenly spun thread which lends almost a clouded effect to the ground it is worked on. The patterns of Burano lace are usually composed of a simple coral spray or a floral disc motif, outlined with a heavier thread overcast with a sparsely worked buttonhole stitch. Both the clouded effect and the simple coral sprays reflect the legendary solidified foam of the mermaids.

Continuing with our lace travels around the world, we reach Flanders, whose lace-makers had developed some of the finest laces in existence. The progress of their lace-making efforts was roughly contemporary and parallel to that of the Venetians. Good lace was made and worn in Flanders as far back as the fifteenth century although records, except for the occasional evidence found in paintings of that century, fail to throw very much light on exactly when lace-making did start in the area. Existing documents show, however, that it was a thriving industry by the second half of the sixteenth century.

According to these documents, early attempts had been made in Flanders to imitate the designs of Venice and Genoa. This early work, however, soon acquired a distinct quality and characteristic of its own, again largely reflecting the temperament and personality of the people who were making it. The hard-working and industrious Flemish, certainly more serious and less flamboyant by nature than the Italians, excelled in creations that required an infinite amount of patience and painstaking skill, and it is truly the fineness and delicacy of their work that has made it so justly famous.

An example of the great detail in which the Flemish people delighted is one of their earliest preserved pieces of bobbin lace, a bedspread made in 1599 in honor of the marriage of Albert and Isabella, Archduke and Archduchess of Brabant. The bedspread is now in the collection of the Brussels Museum of Art and History. Into its countless squares are worked images of Isabella and the Archduke, the King and Queen of Spain, the King and Queen of France, and St. Gudule, the patron saint of Brussels, between an angel and the devil, as well as numerous other saints and symbols. One of the most fascinating aspects of this whole tremendous undertaking was the

Punto Avorio. Italian, seventeenth century. The Metropolitan Museum of Art, New York (Rogers Fund, 1909)

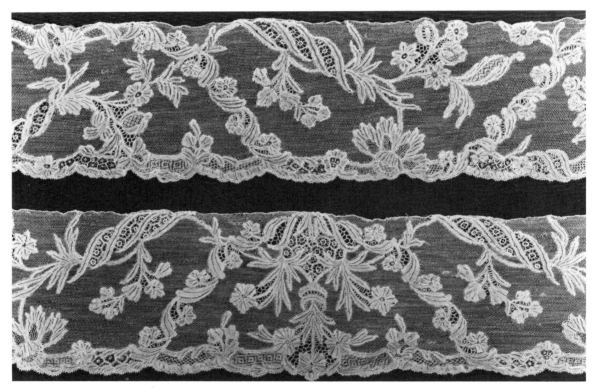

Point de Burano borders. Italian, eighteenth century. Cooper-Hewitt Museum of Decorative Arts and Design, Smithsonian Institution, New York

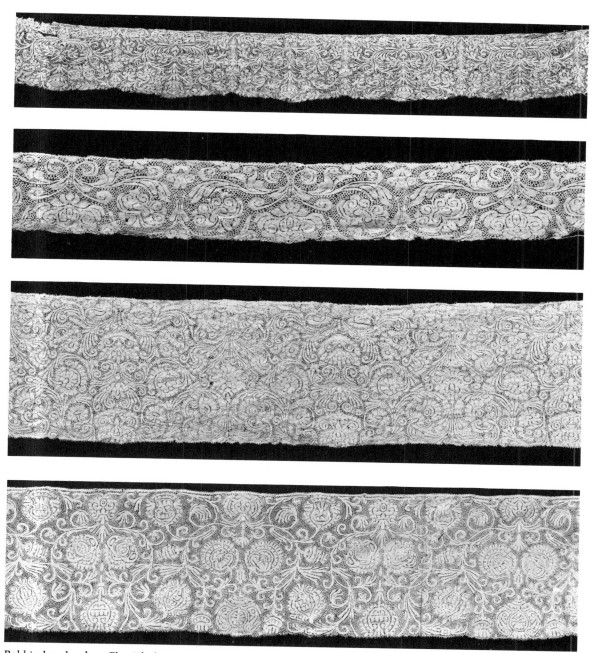

Bobbin lace borders. Flemish, late seventeenth century. Victoria and Albert Museum, London (Crown Copyright)

use of minutely detailed human figures incorporated into the design, a type of work which had never gained much prominence in any of the early Italian laces. It was just this type of involved detail in some of the Flemish work that required such effort as that of one worker who needed fifteen hours a day for ten months to complete a single pair of Binche cuffs.

In the opinion of the experts, who base their choice on design, quality of thread, and expertise of workmanship, point de Gaze and other Brussels laces and the Brabant pieces are the finest of the Flemish work, those of Mechlin and Antwerp come next, and finally the Valenciennes and Binche varieties. Point de Malines, the name of Mechlin lace made at Antwerp, was highly favored abroad, particularly in England, where Queen Mary and

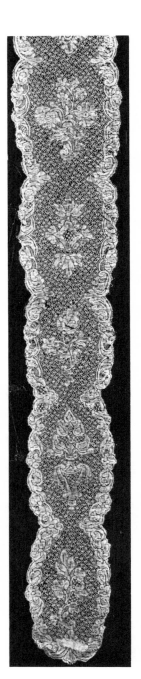

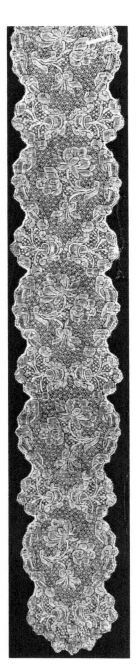

Binche cap crown; *right*, two lappets. Early eighteenth century, origin unknown. Victoria and Albert Museum, London (Crown Copyright)

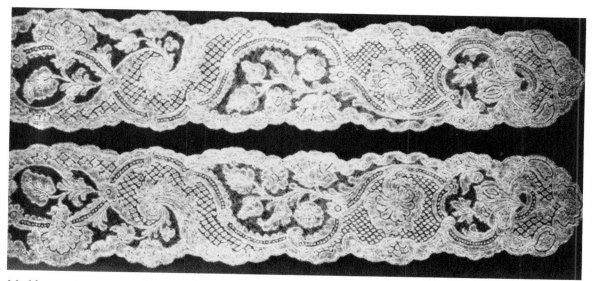

Mechlin, or Malines, pair of lappets. Flemish, early eighteenth century. Cooper-Hewitt Museum of Decorative Arts and Design, Smithsonian Institution, New York (Ex coll. Richard C. Greenleaf)

Brussels point de Gaze fan mount. Mid-nineteenth century. Victoria and Albert Museum, London (Crown Copyright)

Point de Gaze linen and lace handkerchief. Belgian, late nineteenth century. The Metropolitan Museum of Art, New York (Bequest of Catherine D. Wentworth, 1948)

Valenciennes bobbin lace and linen handkerchief. Belgian, late nineteenth century. The Metropolitan Museum of Art, New York (Bequest of Catherine D. Wentworth, 1948)

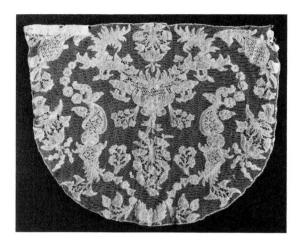

Point d'Angleterre cap crown. Flemish, mid-eighteenth century. The Metropolitan Museum of Art, New York (The Mabel Metcalf Fahnestock Collection, gift of Ruth Fahnestock Schermerhorn and Faith Fahnestock, 1933)

Queen Anne wore a great deal of it. It was a lace which was also especially admired by Napoleon who, when he first saw the exquisite spire of the Antwerp Cathedral, exclaimed, "C'est comme la dentelle de Malines!"—"It is like the lace of Malines!"

Moving along to France, we come to the last of the important lace-making centers to have developed, and to one of the greatest. It is a little difficult to understand why the people of that nation, known to be creative and usually very avant garde, were quite willing to import most of the lace they used until that time when, not too early in the recorded history of lace-making, Catherine de Medici married King Henry II and brought with her from Italy her enthusiasm for the delicate finery and her skilled lace workers whose

training she had sponsored in her native country long before her marriage to the King of France.

With that great woman as their inspiration and sponsor, however, the French very quickly set about learning everything she had to teach them, and before very long there seemed to be no limit to the extent of their enthusiasm and no control on their desire to make and to use as much lace as they possibly could. They copied their Queen's patterns at first, and paid minute attention to every detail of the work that was being done by the skilled craftsmen she had brought with her. Fascinated by all her beautiful finery, they emulated everything they saw and very soon thereafter they began to innovate patterns and designs. The French became known as the pacesetters of lace fashion in Europe, a reputation they maintained throughout the era of the handmade lace industry, and even to this very day when the machine-made laces of France are considered to be among the finest in the world.

The preceding chapter traced the development of the love for lace in France and the progress of the lace-making art there. Louis XIV and his shrewd minister, Colbert, raised France as a lace-making nation to its greatest and most magnificent height. Colbert, in particular, grasped the importance of such an industry to the French economy, and it was during his ministry that centers were set up in Alençon, Argentan, Sedan, and Rheims, among several other areas.

By royal decree, many of the fine laces that

Point de France flounce, Sedan type. French, late seventeenth century. The Metropolitan Museum of Art, New York (The Mabel Metcalf Fahnestock Collection, gift of Ruth Fahnestock Schermerhorn and Faith Fahnestock, 1933)

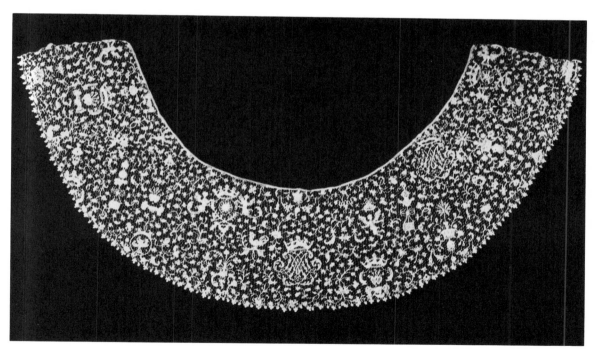

Point de France bertha. Monogram of Marie Therese and royal emblem. French, late seventeenth century. Victoria and Albert Museum, London (Crown Copyright)

Detail of point de France flounce. French, eighteenth century. Corcoran Gallery of Art, Washington, D.C. (W. A. Clark Collection)

Detail of point d'Alençon flounce. French. Corcoran Gallery of Art, Washington, D.C.

Detail of point d'Argentan flounce. French, mid-eighteenth century. Victoria and Albert Museum, London (Crown Copyright)

Detail of point d'Argentan flounce. French, mid-eighteenth century. Corcoran Gallery of Art, Washington, D.C.

Black Chantilly lace fan. French, late nineteenth century. Victoria and Albert Museum, London (Crown Copyright)

were being made at that time, whether copied or original, became known as point de France, and still others as point Colbert. Actually, it is not known just when the laces of Alençon and Argentan, for example, ceased to be termed point de France and became known by the name of the cities in which they were made, although, according to some records, an inventory of 1723 is the last to have mentioned point de France, while the first mention of point d'Argentan appeared in 1738 and of point d'Alençon in 1741.

Among the first of the fine needlepoint laces to have been produced under royal patronage in France were those of Alençon, which were rather close copies of the Italian gros point de Venise. Before long, however, the French developed their own image in their lace-making, even when they were copying the work of others. They increased the number of brides in their work until these formed a large hexagonal mesh, and they used this mesh as a background for the exquisite new patterns they began to design. Point d'Alençon soon became a very distinct and individual type of lace with special characteristics of its own, and one that was considered to be perhaps the best of all the French needlepoint lace.

The lace that was being made at nearby

Argentan was quite similar to that made at Alençon, although it was not considered to be quite so fine. The patterns in both of these types were crisp, clear, and bold, and in each the design of the brides contributed a great deal to its unique quality.

Since the only two true types of lace, that which was made with the needle only and that made with needle and bobbins, had already really been established, there could be no new method worked in France, the late-comer to the industry. At this period in the lace-making history of the world, only the addition of new characteristics, new designs, and a new touch plus the industrial prowess and style consciousness of the French could possibly have established them as one of the great lace-making nations. Aiding their rapid progress was the fact that many workers in the prominent French lace-making cities had already been touched with a knowledge of the lace-making art practiced by other countries. This was so because at one time many of the northern French cities were part of Flanders. Valenciennes, for instance, had been a town in the Flemish province of Hainaut until 1678, when it became a part of France. Lille, another of the great French lace-making centers, had also belonged to Flanders until about that time. Ancestors of people in both these communities had early learned the art.

Among some of the French innovations affecting the existing needlepoint and bobbin laces were those of the Chantilly pieces. These were unusual in that they were made of black

Lace shawl

or white silk, a new thought in lace-making and one which survived even the Revolution. In 1805, white silk lace became very fashionable in Paris; and during the Victorian era in England, black Chantilly lace shawls were the rage.

Another special characteristic of the Chantilly laces was the use of elegant festoons and fine bobbin-made fonds in the patterns. The

Lace-Making Around the World **73**

Lille medallion. French, early nineteenth century.
Cooper-Hewitt Museum of Decorative Arts and
Design, Smithsonian Institution, New York (Ex coll.
Richard C. Greenleaf)

Lille laces, which were made in both Lille
and nearby Arrás, closely resembled the
Flemish Mechlin pieces, as did the Lorrain
laces. Here too, however, there was a distinc-
tion: very delicate flowers were attached to
the special réseaux that were being made in
these areas.

Incidentally, while the Lille pieces were
considered rather coarse and strong and somewhat in the category of "pedestrian lace," the
same type of lace in Arrás was made of gold
thread which was a rather unusual material,
used there because Arrás was the great tapestry center in France and workers in that city

were particularly adept at handling gold
thread.

The Valenciennes laces were notably
French in design too, being generously show-
ered with many detached little floral sprays, a
particular pattern that made these pieces especially attractive for articles of personal adornment.

As we travel the world of lace, we must be
mindful that the making of true lace is really
limited to only needlepoint and bobbin types,
and that in just about three centuries lace
developed from an attractive but rather crude
type of embellishment to one of magnificence
and perfection in finely detailed design. As
wholly or partially machine-made laces began
to be substituted for the completely handmade, the lace-making efforts of France could
already do no more than improve upon that
which had already been done. While there was
still a great deal of interest in lace-making and
actually rather some excitement in the creation of new designs, there was not really anything very much that was or could be added
in the way of technical skill.

What remains to be seen in our tour of the
world of lace are other examples of that which
had already been done, yet again touched just
a little with the addition of new details, each
reflecting the personalities and individual
characteristics of those who were doing the
work. Both Spain and England were very interested in the lace-making efforts of other
countries, watching the style trends that were
developing. The lace-makers of both of these

Bobbin lace silk scarf. Spanish, early nineteenth century. The Metropolitan Museum of Art, New York (Gift of Mrs. John C. Gray, 1913)

Black silk lace strip, machine-made. Spanish, nineteenth century. The Metropolitan Museum of Art, New York (Rogers Fund, 1922)

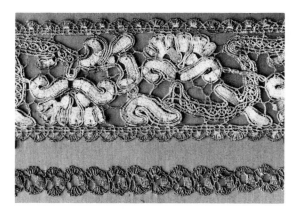

Silver bobbin lace strip. Spanish, seventeenth century. The Metropolitan Museum of Art, New York (Rogers Fund, 1909)

countries, each in their own way, attempted to follow these trends.

Perhaps the greatest stimulus for the Spanish was the marriage of King Louis XIV of France to the Infanta of Spain. It was she who was largely responsible for introducing the lace-making art and the lace fashion trends to the people of her own country, although the nobility, the clergy, and those who were more aware of the activities of the outside world had known of the importance of lace fashion long before. Once this fashion knowledge became available to the Spanish population as a whole, however, they, being of a disposition easily impressed with this type of finery, began to import a great deal of lace and to make some effort of their own to copy what they had imported.

Unfortunately, their efforts in making their own lace were not especially noteworthy. The rather popular Spanish Blonde lace, a product most often made of black silk though labeled blonde because originally it had been made in cream color or white, was one that the Spanish used a lot of for the deep lace flounces on their bright satin skirts and for their mantillas, the national headdress of Spanish women. More of this lace was produced in Chantilly, however, than in Barcelona where the people had made a special effort to at least be able to copy it.

It is of interest to note that the new lace fashions were of such major importance to the people of Spain that, for example, national fashion decreed that ladies had to wear black lace mantillas except at bullfights and other special occasions when they were to wear white; and a woman's mantilla had so great a value that it was legally protected and could never be seized in payment of a debt of any kind.

The story of Spanish lace reflects, perhaps a little sadly, a preference for the "show" rather than the quality of lace. Attempting to copy the needle and bobbin laces of Italy, Flanders, and France, the Spanish lace-making efforts were enthusiastic but a bit more colorful than careful. Most of the pieces they made were quite loosely worked, and the patterns were a little straggling and confused. A good example of this is the attempt to make a needlepoint lace corresponding to the Italian punto in aria. In the Spanish pieces a vase form was always more bulbous in character, and leaves and flowers were inclined to be rounder and flatter

Goya's "Don Manuel Osorio de Zuniga." The Metropolitan Museum of Art, New York
(The Jules S. Bache Collection, 1949)

Punto de Catalina ecclesiastical costume, embroidered in gold thread. Spanish, nineteenth century. The Metropolitan Museum of Art, New York (Gift of Mrs. Nuttall, 1908)

than the delicately curved lines of those of the original pieces. When the carefully drawn Flemish bobbin laces were copied, the patterns were much less meticulously outlined and the delicate scroll motifs often terminated in pomegranates or disc-like flowers set into very loose open-mesh backgrounds.

When new designs were attempted, they were often flamboyant. In some instances the design loosely incorporated the double eagle or lions of Castile alternating with patterns of turreted castles set in a field peopled with rather archaic figures and stylistic birds.

Among the most original of the Spanish laces were *punto de Cataluna,* in which the sun or "sol" pattern dominated the design, and *punto de España.* The latter was most often made of gold thread, the motifs outlined with a series of small gold picots and the foundation worked over with a weaving stitch of polychrome or silver silk.

Though the designs described were free and easy and certainly reflective of the brilliant vivaciousness of the Spanish people, it is obvious that the lace that was made was not at all comparable in quality to the fine work that was being done elsewhere. If this description of the Spanish lace-making effort seems to classify it as second-best, this unfortunately is what it was.

Although English lace work was surely more sober than the Spanish and much of it quite fine in quality, the total effort of those enterprising people in making truly good lace was hampered a great deal by the unavail- ability of fine native thread, and by the more methodical and less imaginative nature of the English people themselves. Their major contribution to the art of lace-making was rather in the spinning of thread for other countries, and in the invention and perfection of the revolutionizing lace-making machines. Chapter 2 told of the love of lace of England's royalty, some of whom were concerned with it only for personal adornment while others, particularly Queen Elizabeth I and, much later, Queen Victoria, saw the possibilities of lace-making as a revenue-producing industry. Both of these monarchs did a great deal to champion that industry.

Politics played perhaps a more important role in England's lace-making history than in the industry's development in most other parts of the world. The very establishment of her lace industry owes its beginning to the influx of continental refugees who poured into England after the middle of the sixteenth century. In 1563, Flemish Protestants fleeing the terrors of the Spanish Inquisition came to England. Among them were many lace workers who settled along the coast of Kent. In 1568, a second group from the Mechlin lace district settled in Bedfordshire and Buckinghamshire, and again in 1572 there was still another influx of foreigners. At this time a group of French refugees emigrated to England to escape the persecution of the Huguenots. Included in their numbers were many who came from some of the important lace-making centers of France.

Goya, "Mayas on a Balcony"

become well supplied with lace workers from other countries who were quietly laying the foundation for a thriving industry for future generations. By the early seventeenth century, the English lace-making industry had become of major commercial importance, as evidenced by one English company's record sale in 1620 of a very large quantity of lace exported to India for the ruler of Golcanda, a major mining center.

A final influx of refugees from France at the time of the revocation of the Edict of Nantes in 1685 brought lace workers once more to England, this time from Chantilly, Alençon and Argentan, each group bringing with it the special knowledge of the techniques in which each of their native areas had specialized. England's lace industry thus thrived largely because of Flemish and French refugees who helped to establish the centers, particularly at Honiton, Buckinghamshire, Bedfordshire, and Devonshire. The work that was done in these areas was good although, in spite of the expertise of the workers, little new was added in the way of design to the patterns that had already been devised, except perhaps for the use of acorns and oak branches which sometimes served as a background for the popular English feather motifs.

Thus it was that, at the time of the accession of Queen Elizabeth to the throne, while foreign markets were still supplying England with laces of gold and silver for royal indulgence and with the more simple bobbin laces used for elaborate neck ruffs, aprons, and the recently introduced lace handkerchief mode of the moment, England herself suddenly had

Elsewhere than in the countries to which our lace travels have taken us, little or no completely handmade lace of any merit or originality was made, and this was so for many obvious reasons. In the United States, for example, some early settlers had brought

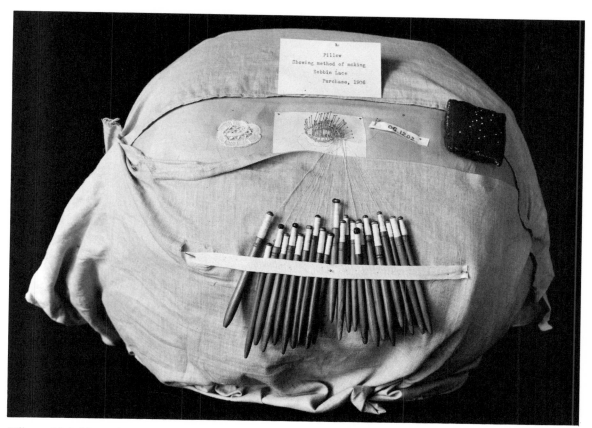

Pillow with bobbins showing method of making Honiton lace. English, nineteenth century. The Metropolitan Museum of Art, New York (Rogers Fund, 1906)

with them a few fine pieces of lace, and those who prospered here managed later to import a little more from Europe. By and large, however, our ancestors were for many years confronted and preoccupied by rugged frontier conditions that made such refined and time-consuming occupations as fine lace-making very much out of the question. Whatever efforts were made seem to have been confined to just a little drawn- and cutwork, and later to the implement lace-making crafts of crocheting and tatting. In addition to being quite attractive, crocheted and tatted pieces were quicker to make, and had the necessary added virtue of durability, since these crafts used much coarser thread and the work could be more easily cared for.

Other countries, however, did experiment

Lace-Making Around the World **81**

Honiton bertha on machine-made net. English, nineteenth century. Victoria and Albert Museum, London (Crown Copyright)

Honiton cuffs. English, late nineteenth or early twentieth century. Victoria and Albert Museum, London (Crown Copyright)

a little more with the art of fine lace-making, but most of the efforts unfortunately were neither very successful nor of long duration. In the Mediterranean area, the Aegean island of Crete did work for a while at a simple type of bobbin lace in which patterns were boldly outlined in color. The silk bobbin lace of Malta was recognizable by its Maltese cross design, a pattern which was later copied to some small degree in the Far East where it had been carried by missionaries. In Morocco, rich in the field of embroidery, some lace work was done, but there it was confined pretty much to coarse, heavily knotted filet patterns,

Buckinghamshire "point" bobbin lace shawl. English, nineteenth century. Victoria and Albert Museum, London (Crown Copyright)

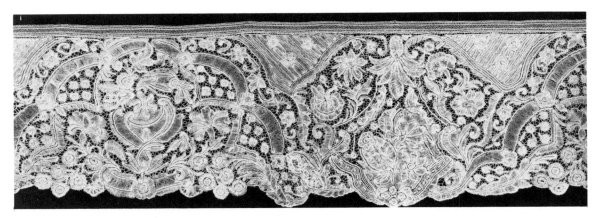

Devon bobbin lace border. English, late eighteenth century. Victoria and Albert Museum, London (Crown Copyright)

designed with the archaic animal motifs which were popular in Spain, and to some very simple needlepoint lace closely resembling the Italian punto Avorio.

Germany, benefiting as did England from the inflow of Flemish and French refugees escaping the various persecutions, also made some early attempts at lace-making. For some reason or other though, aside from the large bobbin lace industry that had been established there in the mid-sixteenth century by Barbara Uttmann (see Chapter 2), and aside from the fact that the German presses were among the first to print lace pattern books, Germany never really did attain very much prominence in the field of lace-making. The little work done consisted of some rather fine drawnwork during the mid-eighteenth century in Dresden. At that time the European fashion of the moment demanded "Dresden ruffles" and "Dresden aprons." Also, some bobbin lace

was made for native headdresses, a lace often referred to as Nuremberg lace, although it very closely resembled the Valenciennes and Mechlin work, but done with coarse thread which resulted in a much less delicate texture; and some peasant laces in central and southern Germany, these pieces rather resembling the lace of Russia, being of the serpentine braid type, coarsely worked in crudely drawn patterns.

Russia had experimented with the making of fine lace when Peter the Great, returning home from a trip through the Continent, founded the first Russian lace factory at Novgorod at the beginning of the eighteenth century. Some silk bobbin lace was made there, but the manufacture lasted only a short while, and no really fine lace has been made in Russia since. More suitable to the Russian temperament were a number of coarse bobbin laces made by the peasants. These often had

Burato network border. Probably German, sixteenth century. The Metropolitan Museum of Art, New York
(Rogers Fund, 1920)

Peasant lace border of linen and gold thread on gold
thread ground, bobbin lace edging. Russian, nineteenth century. The Metropolitan Museum of Art,
New York (Gift of Susan Dwight Bliss, 1948)

Tonder bobbin lace bridal veil. Danish, eighteenth
century. The Metropolitan Museum of Art, New York
(Rogers Fund, 1921)

red or blue threads running through them for a touch of gay color. They were not terribly festive and were used primarily for trimming aprons, blouses, and household linens.

Peasant laces are also the story of lace-making in the Scandinavian countries. In Denmark the peasant Tonder lace, worked on coarse muslin, was the most popular one made. In Sweden a loosely woven gold gimp or braid had been made as early as the sixteenth century, but the native people preferred a coarse, rather simple type of cutwork and a loosely made crude form of bobbin lace. These pieces were used largely for the trimming of household linens, aprons, and other simple clothing.

Our last stop now is a visit to Ireland, the rugged country where not much had ever been done in the way of lace-making until the nineteenth century, when some rather unusual and exquisite work was done. The making of the lovely Irish patterns marks a transition point between the old and the new in the whole story of lace. In the course of time bits and pieces of the various methods of lace-making had filtered through to Ireland pretty much as it did to other countries.

Carrickmacross, the beautiful needlerun lace named for the town in which it was made, is considered to be the oldest authentic Irish lace, dating to 1820 when it had been originated by Mrs. Gray Porter, the wife of the Rector of Dunnamoyne. Limerick lace, done with a chain stitch and a crochet hook on machine-made net, was another delicate and lovely type of Ireland's early work, and

Youghal Point, the only true Irish needlepoint lace ever made, had been taught to the people by Mother Mary Ann Smith of Youghal's Presentation Convent. Having procured an interesting piece of Italian lace from a wandering peddler, she mastered the art of making it herself and passed her knowledge on to the children in the convent school.

None of these techniques were ever really practiced to any extent, however, until the time of the dread potato famine in 1846. Lace-making started as a relief measure then and culminated in the creation of some of the most beautiful lace the world has ever known.

Among the many who offered suggestions as to ways in which the Irish might alleviate their financial woes were several who suggested the business of lace-making. Imaginative by nature, spurred on by necessity, and grateful for the interest that was shown by those who heard of their plight and wanted to help, the Irish people were eager to do what they could with the knowledge they already had and with the new skills being taught to them. Among these was the very new art of making crocheted lace, the lace for which they were to become so very famous. This technique was first taught them by some ladies of the English nobility who had recently learned it from a Mlle. Riego de la Blanchardière of France, the woman credited for having initiated it and for having succeeded in imitating with her little sliver-thin crochet hook some of the lovely old Venetian needlepoint lace designs.

With the suggestions, then, of their many

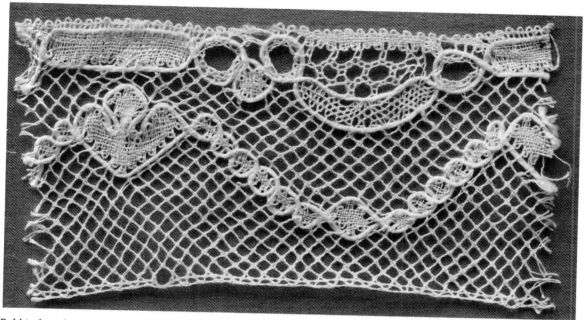

Bobbin lace fragment. Swedish, nineteenth century. The Metropolitan Museum of Art, New York (Gift of the Society for Women's Work, Stockholm, through Miss M. T. Johnston, 1908)

Baby's shirt. Swedish, twentieth century. The Metropolitan Museum of Art, New York (Purchase, 1908)

Carrickmacross scarf. Irish, nineteenth century. The Metropolitan Museum of Art, New York (Gift of Mrs. Lewis L. Strauss, 1961)

Limerick child's dress, machine net embroidered in Tambour stitch. Irish, nineteenth century. The Metropolitan Museum of Art, New York (Gift of Ann Payne Blumenthal, 1937)

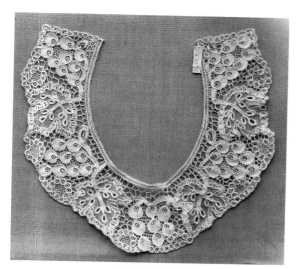

Youghal needlepoint collar in grapevine pattern. Irish, nineteenth century. The Metropolitan Museum of Art, New York (Gift by Subscription, 1909. Blackborne Collection)

friends, the earlier knowledge they had, the learning of new skills, and the support of Queen Victoria herself who specially wore lace to promote the fashion for it and to sponsor the growth of the industry, the Irish learned quickly and soon became one of the most renowned lace-making countries in the world. "Cottage industries" were set up throughout Ireland, the work being done in the workers' homes, rather than in organized lace-making schools or centers. The people worked prolifically, and did indeed help to alleviate their economic distress with the new industry they had established.

It was because of their economic disaster

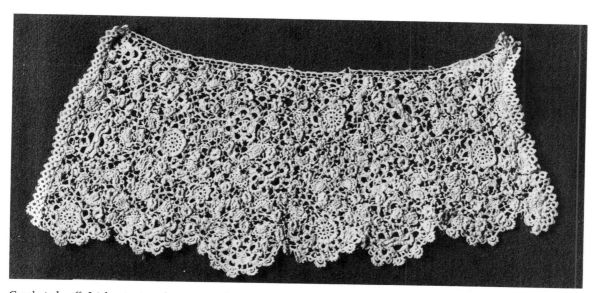

Crocheted cuff. Irish, nineteenth century. The Metropolitan Museum of Art, New York (Gift of Mrs. H. McKnight Moore, in memory of her mother, Mrs. James Snydam, 1924)

that the Irish turned naturally to the lace-making methods that could be worked more quickly than the conventional techniques involved in the making of needlepoint and bobbin laces. Except for the Youghal needlepoint pieces which became practically a native product through the convent schools, most of their work was concentrated on the needlerun and crocheted laces, both of which, though very fine, were quickly made.

"Irish crochet" is an outstanding example of this. Though made quickly with a crochet hook, the use of fine thread and the imaginative designs created by the Irish made this work a worthy rival of the "true" laces. Enthusiastic about this new art, the Irish began adding their own designs to those which had been given to them. Indeed, the vivid imagination of the workers in creating new designs was nothing less than inspired. Three-leafed shamrocks and roses blossomed forth on lacy backgrounds, and many other exciting new patterns were transferred into lovely lace effects.

Their creative imagination was stimulated by the combination of their emergency crisis and the new art that had been taught to them, and the earlier and more delicate of their work was equaled only by that which they did later. Though this work became less fine in detail as the demand for it grew, it became even more imaginative in design.

Though the making of real lace largely came to an end more than a century ago, the second part of this book will tell of the lovely delicate laces that are being made in our time. Certainly not nearly as fine as the earlier pieces that have been described, they are pieces of interest and charm and so much more in keeping with our way of living.

PART II

Patterns

A Foreword

We come now to the contemporary part of this book, the portion which includes several lace designs of the type that many of us enjoy making and using today. The patterns are worked in some of the different media which are fun for those of us who are just a little short of time and patience, yet more than happy to "hobby along" with some interesting handwork that affords us some moments of relaxation and offers us a means of personal self-expression. Many of the models are quite fragile and delicate in nature, and while others are a little more coarse, all are quite lovely and fall into the category of twentieth-century lace-making.

To those "lacers" who may differ with this opinion and may even feel that the original true art is being rather belittled, we must contend that while we do indeed fully appreciate and share their interest in striving to preserve the beautiful needlepoint and bobbin lace-making techniques of centuries ago, our own premise in presenting these patterns is certainly also accompanied with very valid reasoning. It is better to do what we can and to enjoy what we are doing, rather than to be critical of our efforts because we feel that they are not quite good enough, or to abstain completely from any endeavor of this kind because the modern way of living does not permit the time to indulge in the practice of the skills necessary to produce the very fine work.

The first three of the following chapters on various types of things to make are picture-gallery chapters. The first shows lovely designs for a variety of versatile motifs, edgings and insertions; the second, pictures of things to make for the home; and the third, fashions of our day. The models shown in these are crocheted, knitted, tatted, or made of hairpin lace, and subsequent chapters give instructions for making the things that have been shown, with very clear "how-to" directions for working each of the different techniques and each of the patterns. Suggestions are given, too, in some instances, as to how your own individual designs may be employed to vary the models shown.

In collecting patterns for this part of the book, every effort was made to select items that are appealing and of interest to us now, but also rather timeless in their own way. One of the tablecloths was designed almost a hundred years ago, yet it is as attractive and desirable a home accessory now as it was at the time it was made. The fashions, very much in vogue today, are classic in design, and aside from the possible shortening or lengthening of a hemline, they are things that we will enjoy wearing for many years to come. We are very grateful to those individuals and companies who are most knowledgeable and most involved in the world of needlework arts and crafts today, and who have been very cooperative in offering for use in this book the best of the lace work that they have compiled during the past many years. Special thanks for patterns and instructions are extended to the American Thread Company, Emile Bernat & Sons, the Brunswick Worsted Mills, Coats & Clark, the D.M.C. Corporation, Reynolds Yarns, the Scovill Manufacturing Company, the Bernhard Ulmann Company, and the William Unger Company.

 # FOUR

Edgings, Insertions, and Motifs

The "trimming" items in this chapter have been designed primarily for the purpose of lending a decorative finish to something which is usually complete unto itself but grows more attractive with a little added touch. Traditionally this type of ornamentation has been used most often on handkerchiefs, tablecloths, bed linens, and fancy show towels.

Edgings, most often straight at the top only, are used as a border or final finish; insertions, shaped the same at the top and bottom and usually straight at these edges, are generally set between two tiers of some woven design to create a striped or tiered effect. Motifs, on the other hand, have always served a dual purpose: the first to be used as a form of appliqué work or as an interesting small insertion set within whatever the finished item may be; and the second as a

very integral part of whatever it is that is being made, a series of motifs joined together, for instance, forming the whole of a lovely bedspread or tablecloth.

The particular appeal of this type of work is that it offers so much choice to anyone who is interested in doing it. There is no limit to the number or variety of things that can be made more attractive with a little handmade trim, nor are there any bounds on the extent or the amount of trim, or the way in which it can be used. We have spoken of how personal and household linens can be enhanced in this way, and the patterns show several designs very applicable for this use. A change, however, in the weight, texture, or color of the thread or yarn used and a change of needle size can transpose any of the designs shown into very contemporary trimmings which can be used most effectively to decorate

95

VALENTINE BOUQUET

A dinner cloth made of crocheted motifs

Directions appear on page 128

VICTORIANA

A dinner cloth made with a knitted insertion and edging

Directions appear on page 169

dresses and skirts and sweaters, and even the throw pillows and rugs in our homes. Motifs can be enlarged and worked with different yarns and needles to become the stunning parts of the whole of a very modern placemat set or coverlet. One's imagination can play endlessly in this area.

At the beginning of this chapter are shown

a motif pattern, an edging, and an insertion, and also the way in which each of these has been incorporated into the making of a lovely finished piece. This approach will help stimulate your own thoughts by showing you how some of these particular designs have been used and by suggesting things that you might want to make with other patterns.

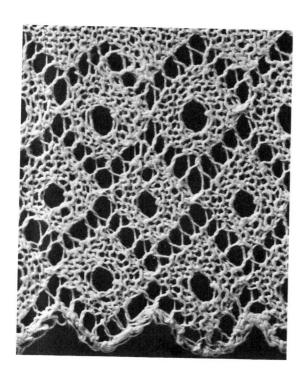

WHEAT EDGING

*A crocheted edging worked to fit a circle, a square,
or a straight edge, used with a wide border, a narrow
border, or no border at all*

Directions appear on page 129

SMALL FLOWERS

A tatted motif

Directions appear on page 194

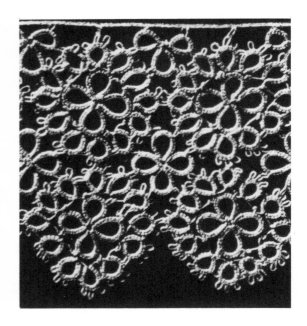

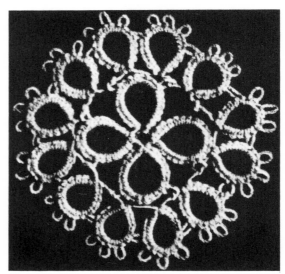

DELICATE TRACERY

A strip of lace made of tatted motifs

Directions appear on page 194

IRISH ROSE

A crocheted edging

Directions appear on page 131

CLOVERLEAF

A tatted motif

Directions appear on page 194

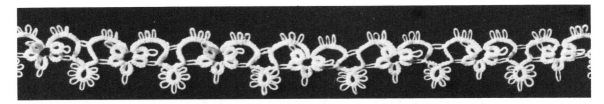

DAINTY FLOWERS AND LACE

A tatted edging

Directions appear on page 195

MILLE FLEURS

A tatted edging

Directions appear on page 195

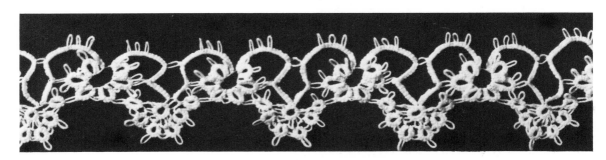

FALLING SNOWFLAKES

A tatted edging

Directions appear on page 195

SCALLOPED LACE

A tatted edging

Directions appear on page 196

LACY FANS

A crocheted insertion

Directions appear on page 132

Edgings, Insertions, and Motifs **101**

SCROLLS

A crocheted insertion

Directions appear on page 133

CLOUDS

A tatted insertion

Directions appear on page 196

FLORAL FANTASY

A tatted insertion

Directions appear on page 197

FIVE

Home Decor

The collection of home decor designs shown consists of pieces which have been proven favorites through the decades and are as attractive and desirable today as they were many years ago. The doilies and centerpieces, tablecloths and bedspreads are indeed lovely and quite fragile in design. While they are not easy to make, the work involved is very interesting and the reward for having made the effort is one that comes only with the creation of any heirloom piece whether it be a painting, a piece of sculpture, or a fine hand-wrought silver ring. The designs are shown in each of the four media so popular and appropriate for lace-making today. Although very clearly defined directions for working them are given, the amount of detail involved is rather more suited to the experienced craftsman than to the beginner. While text and illustrations are provided for each of the crafts, it is recommended that those just starting out with a new needlework hobby begin on some simpler project, with the anticipation that with a little more experience one will be able to make any of the pieces from our collection.

MALTESE

A hairpin lace centerpiece

Directions appear on page 153

WILD CALLA

A crocheted centerpiece

Directions appear on page 133

MILLPOND

A knitted centerpiece

Directions appear on page 171

KALEIDOSCOPE

A knitted doily

Directions appear on page 175

MEDALLION

A knitted centerpiece

Directions appear on page 174

Home Decor   **107**

FLOWER FROST

A tatted centerpiece

Directions appear on page 197

CATHEDRAL WINDOW

A crocheted dinner cloth

Directions appear on page 136

MOUNTAIN MEADOW

A crocheted tablecloth

Directions appear on page 137

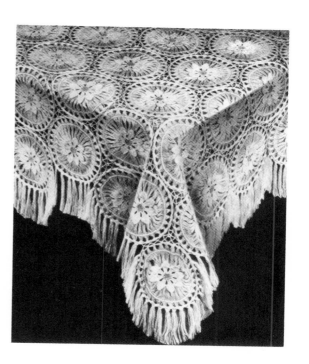

LACE CIRCLES

A hairpin lace tablecloth

Directions appear on page 156

PURITAN

A crocheted bedspread

Directions appear on page 138

MOSAIC ROSE

A crocheted bedspread

Directions appear on page 140

LILY POND
A knitted bedspread
Directions appear on page 177

LACE DIAMONDS
A knitted carriage throw
Directions appear on page 179

PINEAPPLE PARFAIT

A crocheted afghan

Directions appear on page 142

SUNBURST
A hairpin lace afghan and pillow
Directions appear on page 157

FLORAL PUFFS
A hairpin lace afghan
Directions appear on page 158

 # SIX

Fashion

These things to wear represent a collection of garments typical of lace fashions today. Some of the pieces are crocheted, some are knitted, and others are made of hairpin lace. Included is some finery for a very young baby as well as classic fashion designs for women, some of which range from size 8 to size 20. All the patterns, being made of yarn rather than fine thread, are relatively simple to make, and although the styles are quite in vogue today, many of them were designed several years ago. It is the soundness of the designs themselves that has allowed them to maintain their appeal through the years in very much the same way as it will keep them fashionable for many more years to come, needing only perhaps the lengthening or shortening of a hemline to accommodate them to the particular style of the day. The selection of patterns was made with this thought in mind, thus making the effort to work them truly worthwhile.

SCALLOPS OF LACE
A hairpin lace baby layette
Directions appear on page 159

DELICATE VINES
A hairpin lace scarf
Directions appear on page 161

INTERMEZZO
A crocheted shawl
Directions appear on page 144

TOSCA

A hairpin lace stole

Directions appear on page 161

NANETTE

A crocheted triangular shawl

Directions appear on page 146

LILIOM

A hairpin lace shawl

Directions appear on page 162

118 Patterns

PINWHEELS

A hairpin lace shawl

Directions appear on page 164

TEARDROPS

A knitted shell

Directions appear on page 181

BOUQUET

A hairpin lace skirt

Directions appear on page 165

CHANTILLY

A knitted shell

Directions appear on page 182

Fashion **121**

WHISPER
A knitted shell
Directions appear on page 180

CHAMPAGNE
A knitted shell
Directions appear on page 183

CANDY CANE
A knitted slipover
Directions appear on page 184

MIA
A crocheted slipover
Directions appear on page 148

LACE SQUARES
A crocheted dress
Directions appear on page 150

OPEN STRIPES
A knitted dress
Directions appear on page 188

124 Patterns

MONIQUE
A knitted cardigan
Directions appear on page 186

ELEGANCE
A knitted dress
Directions appear on page 189

Fashion **125**

SEVEN

Crochet Directions

HOW TO CROCHET
THE FOUNDATION CHAIN

Knot a loop onto hook. Holding hook in your right hand, the end of yarn extending from the loop in your left hand and the main length of yarn over the index finger of your left hand, * place main length over hook, then draw the yarn and hook through the loop (1st stitch), repeat from * for the desired number of stitches on your foundation chain. Any pattern stitch may be worked on this foundation chain. Turning chains are worked in the same way, and where chain stitches are indicated in a pattern stitch, they are also done in the same way, using the last loop worked as the first one through which your yarn and hook are drawn.

THE STITCH

All stitches are composed of two parts, the top and the base. The top remains the same in all stitches, and the base varies in height according to the stitch being used. All stitches should be worked through both loops of the top unless otherwise specified.

126

THE SLIP STITCH

Insert hook in stitch, yarn over hook and draw through stitch and through loop on hook.

THE SINGLE CROCHET

Insert hook in stitch, yarn over hook and draw through stitch, yarn over and draw through remaining 2 loops on hook.

THE HALF DOUBLE CROCHET

Yarn over hook, insert hook in stitch, yarn over and draw through the stitch, yarn over and draw through remaining 3 loops on hook.

THE DOUBLE CROCHET

Yarn over hook, insert hook in stitch, yarn over and draw through stitch, yarn over and draw through 2 loops on hook, yarn over and draw through remaining 2 loops on hook.

THE TREBLE CROCHET

Yarn over hook twice, insert hook in stitch, yarn over and draw through stitch, (yarn over and draw through 2 loops on hook) 3 times.

A *Double Treble Crochet* is worked as the treble crochet except that yarn is wrapped 3 times over the hook instead of twice, and 2 loops are taken off 4 times instead of 3 times.

A *Triple Treble Crochet* is worked as the treble crochet except that yarn is wrapped 4 times over the hook instead of twice, and 2 loops are taken off 5 times instead of 3 times.

bl	block
ch	chain
d tr	double treble
dc	double crochet
dec	decrease
hdc	half double crochet
hk	hook
inc	increase
lp(s)	loop(s)
rep	repeat
rnd	round
sc	single crochet
sl st	slip stitch
sp(s)	space(s)
st(s)	stitch(es)
tr-cluster	treble cluster
tr c	treble crochet
tr tr	triple treble
*	indicates that directions following are to be repeated as necessary

VALENTINE BOUQUET

As shown on page 96

Design and directions courtesy of Coats & Clark, Inc.

Each motif measures ¾ inch square. Small cloth measures 62 inches square, excluding the border. Large cloth measures 62 x 81 inches, excluding the border.

MATERIALS: Clark's Big Ball Mercerized Crochet Art. B.34, size 20: 19 balls for the small cloth, 22 balls for the large cloth; Art. B.345, size 20: 13 balls for the small cloth, 14 balls for the large cloth. Steel crochet hook No. 9.

First Motif: Starting at center, ch 8. Join with a sl st to form a ring. **Rnd 1:** Ch 4, work (dc, ch 1) 15 times in center of ring. Join last ch 1 to 3rd ch of ch-4. **Rnd 2:** Ch 1, sc in joining, sc in next sp (sc in next dc, sc in next sp) 15 times. Join to 1st sc. **Rnd 3:** Ch 1, sc in joining (draw lp on hk up to measure ¼ inch, thread over and draw through lp on hk, insert hk between ¼ inch lp and the single strand behind it and draw a lp through, thread over and draw through all lps on hk— knot st made. Work another knot st, skip next 3 sc, sc in next sc 7 times; work 1 knot st, then drawing up the lp of the hdc to measure ¼ inch, work in hdc in the 1st sc (long hdc made). **Rnd 4:** Ch 1, sc between double and single lps of hdc just made, * work 2 knot sts, (sc between lp and single strand of next knot st) twice, rep from * around and end with sc in last knot st. Join to 1st sc. **Rnd 5:** Ch 8, * (sc between lp and single strand of next knot st) twice, ch 5, dc in each of the next 2 sc, ch 5, rep from * around and end with 1 dc in the last sc of Rnd 4. Join to 3rd ch of ch-8. **Rnd 6:** Sl st in each of the next 2 ch, sc in lp, * ch 4, holding back on hk the last lp of each tr c, work 3 tr c in the sc just made, thread over and draw through all lps on hk (cluster made), sc in next lp, rep from * around and end with cluster. Join to 1st sc. **Rnd 7:** Ch 1, sc in joining, ch 7, sc in sc between next 2 clusters, * ch 7, in sc between next 2 clusters work a d tr, ch 3 and d tr (ch 7, sc in sc between the next 2 clusters) 3 times. Rep from * around and end with ch 3, tr c in 1st sc to form last lp. **Rnd 8:** Ch 1, sc in lp just formed, (ch 7, sc in next lp) twice, * ch 5, sc in next d tr, ch 15, sc in next d tr (corner lp), ch 5, sc in next lp, (ch 7, sc in next lp) 3 times. Rep from * around. Join last ch 7 to 1st sc. Fasten off.

Second Motif: Work exactly as for 1st motif until 7 rnds have been completed. **Rnd 8:** Ch 1, sc in lp, (ch 7, sc in next lp) twice, ch 5, sc in next d tr, ch 7. Join 2 motifs along one side now as follows: Sl st in any corner lp on 1st motif, ch 7, sc in next d tr on 2nd motif, ch 5, sc in next lp on 2nd motif, (ch 3, sl st in next ch-7 lp on 1st motif, ch 3, sc in next lp on 2nd motif) 3 times, ch 5, sc in next d tr on 2nd motif, ch 7, sl st in next corner lp on 1st motif, ch 7, working on 2nd motif only, sc in next d tr, ch 5, sc in next lp, (ch 7, sc in next lp) 3 times, then starting at * on Rnd 8 of the 1st motif, complete the 2nd motif exactly as for the 1st motif (no more joinings).

Make 19 x 19 motifs for the small cloth, or 19 x 25 motifs for the large cloth, joining as 2nd motif was joined to 1st motif. Where corners meet, join corners to previous joinings.

Border: **Rnd 1:** Attach thread in last ch-7 lp before any corner, work 1 sc, ch 5 and 1 sc in same lp, ch 7, skip next ch-5 lp, * work (sc, ch 7) 3 times and 1 sc in corner lp (3 corner lps), ch 7,** skip next ch-5 lp, work (sc, ch 5, sc and ch 7) 3 times in next lp, skip next ch-5 lp, work (sc, ch 5, sc and ch 7) twice in next lp. Rep from **across to

within next corner lp and end with ch 7. Rep from * around, ending with ch 3 and tr c in 1st sc. **Rnd 2:** Ch 1, work sc, ch 5 and sc in lp just formed, * ch 7, (work sc, ch 5 and sc) 5 times in next ch-7 lp ** ch 7, in next ch-7 lp work sc, ch 5 and sc. Rep from ** across to within last ch-7 lp before the 3 ch-7 corner lps. Rep from * around and end as on Rnd 1. **Rnds 3 and 4:** Ch 1, work sc, ch 5 and sc in lp, * ch 7, work sc, ch 5 and sc in next ch-7 lp. Rep from * around and end as on Rnd 1. Fasten off. Starch lightly and press.

WHEAT EDGING
As shown on page 97

Design and directions courtesy of Coats & Clark, Inc.

MATERIALS: J. & P. Coats Knit-Cro-Sheen or Clark's Big Ball Mercerized Crochet, Art. B.34 or B.345. Steel crochet hook: No. 7 for Knit-Cro-Sheen, No. 8 for size 10 thread, No. 9 for size 20 thread, No. 10 for size 30 thread, No. 12 for size 50 thread, No. 13 for size 70 thread, No. 14 for size 100 thread.

Center Wheat Stalk Strip: Starting at center of narrow edge and leaving a 4-inch end, ch 10. **Row 1 (base of stalk):** In 6th ch from hk work 4 d tr (the 1st 5 ch from hk now count as one d tr), ch 4, d tr, ch 4 and 5 d tr, ch 5, turn. **Rows 2, 3, 4:** Skip 1st d tr, holding back on hk the last lp of each d tr, d tr in each of the next 4 d tr, thread over and draw through all 5 lps on hk, ch 1 tightly to fasten (cluster made and a leaf completed), ch 5, in center d tr work 5 d tr, ch 4, d tr, ch 4 and 4 d tr, * holding last lp back as before, make another d tr in same center d tr, thread over hk 8 times, skip next sp, draw up a lp in next d tr, (thread over and draw through 1st 2 lps on hk) 3 times, then holding last lp back as before, d tr in each of the next 4 d tr (there are 12 lps on hk), thread over and draw through 1st 6 lps on hk to complete cluster (another leaf completed), (thread over and draw through 1st 2 lps on hk) 5 times to complete sp, thread over and draw through remaining 2 lps to complete a d tr over the center d tr of previous row, ch 5, turn. **Row 5:** Skip 1st d tr, cluster over next 4 d tr, ch 5, 5 d tr in center d tr, then work from * to end of 2nd row, ch 5, turn. **Row 6 (top of stalk):** Skip 1st d tr, cluster over next 5 d tr (bud made and stalk completed). Wheat stalk consists of 4 leaves on each side and a bud at top. Ch 9 and rep these 6 rows for pattern.

For Straight Strip: Work in pattern for desired length, being sure to end with a bud. Ch 15 at end of last bud. *Note:* If two-color edging is desired, fasten off thread at end of last bud, attach new color to tip of bud, then make the chain.

For Round Strip: Make a strip of 9 stalks, being sure to end with a bud. Ch 13 at end of last bud. Being careful not to twist strip and using 4-inch end, sew starting chain of the 1st stalk and last bud together to form a circle.

For Square Strip: Make a strip of 8 or more stalks, being sure to end with a bud and to have a multiple of 4 stalks. Ch 15 at end of last bud, then form circle as for Round Strip. Place markers evenly spaced around for corners in each of the 4 buds, having the 1st marker in the bud of the 1st wheat stalk made.

HEADINGS

Straight: **Row 1:** * Working from bud to base of wheat stalk, tr in tip of next leaf, ch 7, dc in tip of next leaf, ch 7, hdc in tip of next leaf, ch 7, sc in tip of next leaf, ch 7, long tr (6 times over hk) in tip of next bud, ch 7, rep from * across ending with ch 7, long tr in 1st ch of starting ch-10, ch 3, turn. **Row 2:** Work 7 dc in next sp, dc in next st, rep from * across ending with 7 dc over 1st 7 ch of last sp, dc in 8th ch. Fasten off.

Round: **Rnd 1:** Work as for 1st row of Straight Heading, working ch 5 (instead of ch 7) throughout and ending with sc in last leaf, ch 7, join with a sl st to 8th ch of ch-13. **Rnd 2:** Ch 3, work as for 2nd row of Straight Heading, working 4 dc (instead of 7 dc) in each sp, join to top of ch-3. Fasten off.

Square: **Rnd 1:** * Starting at the * work as for 1st row of Straight Heading to within one leaf of next marked bud, ch 5, sc in tip of leaf, ch 3, skip marked bud, tr c in tip of next leaf, ch 5, dc in tip of next leaf (corner), ch 7, hdc in tip of next leaf, ch 7, sc in tip of next leaf, ch 7, long tr c in tip of next bud, ch 7, rep from * around, ending with ch 7, join with a sl st to 8th ch of ch-16, ch 3, turn. **Rnd 2:** * Work as for 2nd row of Straight Heading to within next ch-5 sp, 4 dc in ch-5 sp, dc in next tr c, 2 dc in next ch-3 sp, dc in next sc, sl st in next ch-5 sp, ch 3, drop lp off hk, insert hk in 3rd dc preceding sl st and draw dropped lp through, 2 dc in same ch-5 lp, dc in next dc, rep from * around, join to top of ch-3. Fasten off.

EDGINGS

Straight: Attach yarn to 1st ch of starting ch-10, ch 16. **Row 1:** * Working from base of leaf to bud, sc in tip of next leaf, (ch 10, sc in tip of next leaf) 3 times, ch 7, long tr tr (7 times over hk) in tip of next bud, ch 7, rep from * across, ending with a long tr tr in tip of last bud, ch 1, turn. **Row 2:** * In next sp, work (sc, ch 5) twice, sc and ch 3, rep from * across, turn. **Row 3:** * Work dc, ch 3 and dc (V st made) in each of the next 2 ch-5 lps, skip next ch-3 sp, rep from * across, ending with a V st in each of the last 2 ch-5 lps, dc in last sc, ch 1, turn. **Row 4:** In 1st V st sp, work sl, ch 6 and dc, * ch 3, sc in next V st sp, ch 3, V st in next V st sp, rep from * across. Fasten off.

Round: Attach thread to tip of any bud, ch 16. **Rnd 1:** Work as for 1st row of Straight Edging, ending with ch 3, tr c in 9th ch of ch-16 to form last sp. **Rnd 2:** Ch 1, sc in

lp just formed, ch 12, * sc in next lp, ch 12, rep from * around, join and fasten off.

Square: Attach thread to tip of any unmarked bud, ch 16. **Rnd 1:** Work as for 1st row of Straight Edging, working ch 10, (long tr tr and ch 10) 3 times in each of the 4 marked buds and forming the last sp as for Round Edging. **Rnd 2:** Rep 2nd rnd of Round Edging.

IRISH ROSE
As shown on page 99

Design and directions courtesy of American Thread Company

MATERIALS: Puritan Crochet Cotton, size 30. Steel crochet hook No. 10.

Starting at center of one flower, ch 5, join with a sl st to form a ring. Ch 6, dc in ring, * ch 3, dc in ring, rep from * 3 times, ch 3, join in 3rd st of ch. **Rnd 2:** Work (1 sc, 1 hdc, 3 dc, 1 hdc, 1 sc) into each ch-3 sp. **Rnd 3:** * ch 5, sc in back of work between the sc of next 2 petals, rep from * around. **Rnd 4:** Work (1 sc, 1 hdc, 5 dc, 1 hdc, 1 sc) into each ch-5 sp. **Rnd 5:** * Ch 7, sc in back of work between next 2 petals, rep from * around. **Rnd 6:** Work (1 sc, 1 dc, 7 tr c, 1 dc, 1 sc) into each ch-7 sp, join and fasten off.

Joining: Attach thread in center of any petal, * ch 7, thread over hk, insert in last tr c of same petal, draw through, thread over and work off 2 lps, thread over hk, insert in 1st tr c of next petal, draw through, thread over and work off 2 lps, thread over and draw through all lps on hk, ch 7, sc in center st of same petal, rep from * around, join. **Rnd 2:** Sl st into lp, ch 3, 2 dc in same sp, then keeping last lp of each dc on hk, thread over and draw through all lps at one time, ch 9, cluster st in same sp (cluster st: thread over hk, insert in sp, draw through and work off 2 lps, * thread over hk, insert in same sp, draw through and work off 2 lps, rep from * once, thread over and draw through all lps at one time), * ch 7, sc in next lp, ch 3, sc in same sp, ch 7, sc in next lp, ch 3, sc in same sp, ch 7, 2 cluster sts with ch 9 between in next lp (corner), rep from * around ending rnd with (ch 7, sc in next lp, ch 3, sc in same sp) twice, ch 7, join. Work a 2nd flower joining it to 1st flower on last row as follows: sl st into lp, ch 3, 2 dc in same sp, then keeping last lp of each dc on hk, thread over and draw through all lps at one time, ch 4, join to corner lp of 1st flower, ch 4, cluster st in same lp of 2nd flower, * ch 3, sc in next lp of 1st flower, ch 3, sc in next lp of 2nd flower, ch 3, sc in same sp, rep from * once, ch 3, sc in next lp of 1st flower, ch 3, cluster st in next lp of 2nd flower, ch 4, join to next corner lp of 1st flower, ch 4, cluster st in same lp of 2nd flower and complete rnd same as for 1st flower. Join as many flowers as desired in same manner.

Heading: Attach thread in corner lp of 1st flower, ch 10, 2 sc in next ch-7 lp, * ch 7, 2 sc in next ch-7 lp, ch 7, 2 sc in next ch-9 lp, ch 5, dc in joining, ch 5, 2 sc in next ch-7 lp, rep from * across row and fasten off. Attach thread in 3rd st of ch and work * 4 sc in next lp, sc in next sc, ch 4, sl st in top of last sc for picot, sc in next sc, (6 sc in next lp, sc in next sc, picot, sc in next sc) twice, 4 sc in next lp, sc in next dc, ch 4, sl st in top of last sc for picot, rep from * across row and fasten off.

Lower Edge: Attach thread in corner lp of 1st flower, * (ch 8, sc in next ch-7 lp) 3 times, ch 8, sc in joining, rep from * across row, ch 8, turn. **Next Row:** Sc in next lp, (ch 8, sc in next lp) 3 times, * ch 4, sc in next lp, (ch 8, sc in next lp) 3 times, rep from * across row, ch 1, turn. **Next Row:** Work 5 sc, a 4-ch picot and 5 sc over each ch-8 lp, and 5 sc over each ch-4 lp. Fasten off.

LACY FANS
As shown on page 101

Design and directions courtesy of D.M.C. Corporation

MATERIALS: D.M.C. Crochet Cotton, size 30. D.M.C. Big Ball or Crochet Superba, size 30. Steel crochet hook No. 10.

Starting at narrow edge, ch 15. Work (2 dc, ch 2, 2 dc) in 4th ch from hk, (shell made), ch 6, skip 5 ch, (dc, ch 3, dc) in next ch, ch 6, shell in last ch, ch 3, turn. **Row 2:** Shell in ch-2 sp of 1st shell, ch 5, 7 dc in ch-3 sp, ch 5, shell in last shell, ch 3, turn. **Row 3:**

Shell in 1st shell, ch 4, dc in 1st dc of 7-dc group, ch 1 and 1 dc in each of next 6 dc, ch 4, shell in last shell, ch 3, turn. **Row 4:** Shell in 1st shell, ch 1, dc in 1st dc of 7-dc group, (dc in next sp, dc in next dc) 6 times, ch 1, shell in last shell, ch 3, turn. **Row 5:** Shell in 1st shell, ch 6, dc, ch 3 and dc in center dc of completed fan, ch 6, shell in last shell, ch 3, turn. Rep Rows 2 through 5 for desired length.

SCROLLS

As shown on page 102

Design and directions courtesy of D.M.C. Corporation

MATERIALS: D.M.C. Crochet Cotton, size 30. D.M.C. Big Ball or Crochet Superba, size 30. Steel crochet hook No. 10.

1st Ring: Ch 25, join with a sl st to form a ring. **Next Rnd:** Ch 3, work 35 dc in center of ring, ch 1, then work 14 more dc in ring. Join to top of ch-3 and fasten off. **2nd Ring:** Leaving 3″ of thread free, ch 25, then from right side insert end of the 3″ thread down through the ring just made and draw chains through, then join in 1st ch to form a ring, ch 3, work 35 dc in ring just made, ch 1, then work 14 more dc in ring. Join to top of ch-3 and fasten off. Continue to work as many rings as necessary for desired length.

Edging to Be Worked at Top of Rings: With right side of work facing, attach yarn to 1st st, ch 5, * sk 2 sts, work 1 dc in next st,

ch 2, rep from * across length of edging. Fasten off. Work same edging at bottom of strip of rings.

WILD CALLA

As shown on page 105

Design and directions courtesy of Coats & Clark, Inc. Doily measures 14¾ inches in diameter, excluding ruffle.

MATERIALS: Clark's Big Ball Mercerized Crochet, Art. B.34 or B.345, both in size 20. Steel crochet hook No. 9.

Starting at center, ch 4, join with a sl st to form a ring. **Rnd 1:** Ch 1 and work 8 sc in center of ring. Join to 1st sc. **Rnd 2:** Ch 3, dc in joining, (ch 2, 2 dc in next sc) 7 times, ch 2 and join to top of ch-3. **Rnd 3:** Ch 3, dc in next dc, (ch 4, dc in next 2 dc) 7 times, ch 4, join as before. **Rnd 4:** Ch 3, dc in next dc, (ch 6, dc in each of next 2 dc) 7 times, ch 6, join. **Rnd 5:** Ch 3, dc in joining, 2 dc in next dc, (ch 4, 2 dc in next 2 dc) 7 times, ch 4, join. **Rnd 6:** Ch 3, dc in joining, 2 dc in next 3 dc, (ch 2, 2 dc in next 4 dc) 7 times, ch 2, join. **Rnd 7:** Ch 3, dc in joining, 2 dc in each dc around, join. **Rnd 8:** Ch 3, holding back on hk the last lp of each dc, dc in next 3 dc, thread over and draw through all lps on hk (cluster made), * ch 3, 4-dc cluster over next 4 dc, rep from * around, join to tip of first cluster. **Rnd 9:** In next sp work a sl st, ch 3 and 3-dc cluster (starting cluster in sp made), (ch 3, 4-dc cluster in next sp) 6 times, * ch 5, sc in next sp, ch 5, (4-dc cluster in next sp, ch 3) 6 times, 4-dc cluster in next sp, rep from * around, ending with ch 5 and join as before. **Rnd 10:** Starting cluster in next sp (ch 3, 4-dc cluster in next sp) 5 times, ch 5, sc in next lp, ch 2, in next sc work (2 dc, ch 2) twice, sc in next lp, ch 5, (4-dc cluster in next sp, ch 3) 5 times, 4-dc cluster in next sp, rep from * around, ending as before, join. **Rnd 11:** * Cluster in next sp as before, (ch 3, cluster in next sp) 4 times, ch 5, sc in next lp, ch 5, dc in each of next 2 dc, ch 4, dc in each of next 2 dc, ch 5, skip next sp, sc in next lp, ch 5, rep from * around, join. **Rnd 12:** * Cluster in next sp, (ch 3, cluster in next sp) 3 times, ch 5, sc in next lp, ch 5, dc in each of next 2 dc, ch 6, dc in each of next 2 dc, ch 5, skip next sp, sc in next lp, ch 5, rep from * around, join. **Rnd 13:** * Cluster in next sp, (ch 3, cluster in next sp) twice, ch 5, sc in next lp, ch 7, 2 dc in each of next 2 dc, ch 4, 2 dc in each of next 2 dc, ch 7, skip next sp, sc in next lp, ch 5, rep from * around, join. **Rnd 14:** * Cluster in next sp, ch 3, cluster in next sp, ch 7, sc in next lp, ch 7, 2 dc in each of next 4 dc, ch 2, 2 dc in each of next 4 dc, ch 7, skip next sp, sc in next lp, ch 7, rep from * around, join. **Rnd 15:** * Cluster in next sp, ch 9, sc in next lp, ch 9, 2 dc in each of next 16 dc, ch 9, skip next sp, sc in next lp, ch 9, rep from * around, ending with ch 4, d tr in tip of 1st cluster to form last lp. **Rnd 16:** Ch 1, sc in lp just formed, (ch 9, sc in next lp) twice, * ch 5, (cluster over next 4 dc, ch 3) 7 times, cluster over next 4 dc, ch 5, sc in

next lp, (ch 9, sc in next lp) 3 times, rep from * around ending with ch 9, join to 1st sc. Fasten off.

Attach thread to tip of next cluster. **Rnd 17:** * Cluster in next sp, (ch 3, cluster in next sp) 6 times, ch 5, sc in next lp, (ch 9, sc in next lp) 4 times, ch 5, rep from * around, join. **Rnd 18:** * Cluster in next sp, (ch 3, cluster in next sp) 5 times, ch 7, sc in next lp, (ch 9, sc in next lp) twice, ch 5, in next sc work (3-tr cluster in same manner as 1 dc cluster was made, ch 5) twice, (sc in next lp, ch 9) twice, sc in next lp, ch 7, rep from * around, join. **Rnd 19:** * Cluster in next sp, (ch 3, cluster in next sp) 4 times, ch 7, sc in next lp, (ch 9, sc in next lp) twice, ch 5, 3-tr cluster in tip of next cluster (tr-cluster over cluster made), ch 5, sc in next lp, ch 5, tr-cluster over cluster, ch 5, skip next sp, sc in next lp, (ch 9, sc in next lp) twice, ch 7, rep from * around, join. **Rnd 20:** * Cluster in next sp, (ch 3, cluster in next sp) 3 times, ch 7, sc in next lp, (ch 9, sc in next lp) twice, ch 7, tr-cluster over cluster, (ch 7, sc in next lp) twice, ch 7, tr-cluster over cluster, ch 7, skip next sp, sc in next lp, (ch 9, sc in next lp) twice, ch 7, rep from * around, join. **Rnd 21:** * Cluster in next sp, (ch 3, cluster in next sp) twice, ch 7, sc in next lp, (ch 9, sc in next lp) twice, ch 7, tr-cluster over cluster, (ch 7, sc in next lp) 3 times, ch 7, tr-cluster over cluster, ch 7, skip next sp, sc in next lp, (ch 9, sc in next lp) twice, ch 7, rep from * around, join. **Rnd 22:** * Cluster in next sp, ch 3, cluster in next sp, ch 7, sc in next lp (ch 9, sc in next lp) twice, ch 7, tr-cluster over cluster, (ch 7, sc in next lp) twice, ch 5, in next sc work (3-tr cluster, ch 5) twice, (sc in next lp, ch 7) twice, tr-cluster over cluster, ch 7, skip next sp, sc in next lp, (ch 9, sc in next lp) twice, ch 7, rep from * around, join. **Rnd 23:** * Cluster in next sp, ch 7, sc in next lp, (ch 9, sc in next lp) twice, ch 7, tr-cluster over cluster, (ch 7, sc in next lp) twice, ch 5, tr-cluster over cluster, ch 5, sc in next lp, ch 5, tr-cluster over cluster, ch 5, skip next sp, (sc in next lp, ch 7) twice, tr-cluster over cluster, ch 7, skip next sp, sc in next lp (ch 9, sc in next lp) twice, ch 7, rep from * around, ending with ch 3, tr c in tip of 1st cluster to form last lp. **Rnd 24:** Ch 1, sc in lp just formed, (ch 9, sc in next lp) 3 times, * ch 9, tr-cluster over cluster, (ch 7, sc in next lp) twice, ch 7, tr-cluster over cluster, (ch 7, sc in next lp) twice, ch 7, tr-cluster over cluster, ch 7, skip next sp, (sc in next lp, ch 7) twice, tr-cluster over cluster, skip next sp, (ch 9, sc in next lp) 6 times, rep from * around, ending with ch 4, d tr in 1st sc to form last lp. **Rnd 25:** Ch 1, sc in lp just formed, (ch 9, sc in next lp) 3 times, * ch 9, tr-cluster over cluster, (ch 4, 2-tr cluster in tip of cluster just made) twice—cluster chain made, (sc in next lp, ch 4, 2-tr cluster in sc just made, ch 4, 2-tr cluster in tip of cluster just made—another cluster chain made) twice, tr-cluster over cluster (work a cluster chain, sc in next lp) 3 times, work a cluster chain, tr-cluster over cluster, skip next sp, (work a cluster chain, sc in next lp) twice, work a cluster chain, tr-cluster over cluster, skip next sp, (ch 9, sc in next lp) 5 times, rep from * around, forming last lp as before. **Rnd 26:** Ch 1, sc in lp, (ch 9, sc in next lp) 3 times, * ch 9, tr-cluster over cluster, (make a cluster chain, sc in center of next cluster chain) 10 times, make a cluster chain, tr-cluster chain, tr-cluster over cluster, skip next sp, (ch 9, sc in next lp) 4 times, rep from * around ending with ch 9, join to 1st sc. **Rnd 27:** Sl st in next 4 ch, sc in lp, (work a cluster chain, sc in next lp) twice, * work a cluster chain, tr-cluster over cluster, (make a cluster chain, sc in center of next cluster chain) 11 times, work a cluster chain, tr-cluster over cluster, skip next lp, (make a cluster chain, sc in next lp) 3 times, rep from * around, ending with tr-cluster over cluster, ch 4, holding lps back as for previous clusters, work 2 tr c in tip of cluster just made, 3 tr c in 1st sc and complete a cluster, thus forming the last cluster chain. **Rnd 28:** Ch 1, * sc in center of cluster chain, ch 7, rep from * around, join to 1st sc, fasten off.

Ruffle: **1st Rnd:** Work (sc, ch 9) 5 times in each lp around to within last lp. In last lp work (sc, ch 9) 4 times, ch 4, d tr in 1st sc. **Next 6 Rnds:** Ch 1, sc in lp just formed, * ch 9, sc in next lp, rep from * around, forming last lp of 1st 5 rnds as before and ending last rnd with ch 9, join to 1st sc. **Rnd 8:** Ch 1, * sc in lp, ch 4, tr c in sc just made, ch 4, tr c in tr c just made, rep from *

around. Join and fasten off. Starch piece
lightly and press.

CATHEDRAL WINDOW

As shown on page 108

*Design and directions courtesy of American Thread
Company*

Each motif measures 5 inches. Cloth measures approximately 61 x 76 inches.

MATERIALS: Puritan Mercerized Crochet Cotton: 46 250-yd. balls. Steel crochet hook No. 8.

Motifs (Make 180): Ch 8, join with a sl st
to form a ring. Ch 3, work 19 dc in center
of ring, join in 3rd st of ch. **Rnd 2:** Ch 7,
skip 1 dc, dc in next dc, * ch 4, skip 1 dc, dc
in next dc, rep from * 7 times, ch 4, sl st in
3rd st of ch. **Rnd 3:** Ch 1, sc in same sp, *
(2 sc, ch 3 and 2 sc) in next lp, sc in next
dc, rep from * around. **Rnd 4:** Ch 1, sc in
same sp, * 7 dc (shell) in next ch-3 lp, skip 2
sc, sc in next sc, rep from * around and end
with 7 dc in last ch-3 lp, join in 1st sc. **Rnd 5:**
Sl st in center st of shell, * ch 7, sl st in
center st of next shell, rep from * around.
Rnd 6: Ch 5, dc in 2nd st of ch-7 lp, * ch 2,
skip 1 st, dc in next st, rep from * around,
ch 2, join in 3rd st of ch (40 sps). **Rnd 7:**
Sl st in 1st sp, ch 5, 2 tr c cluster st in same
sp (2 tr c cluster st: keeping last lp of each
tr c on hk, work 2 tr c in same sp, thread over
and work off all lps at one time), * ch 5, skip
1 sp, sc in next sp, ch 5, 2 tr c cluster st in
same sp, rep from * around and end with ch
5, skip 1 sp, join (20 cluster sts). **Rnd 8:** Sl

st in top of 1st cluster st, * ch 7, sl st in top of
next cluster st, rep from * around. **Rnd 9:**
Ch 4, skip 1 st of ch, dc in next st, * ch 1,
skip 1 st, dc in next st, rep from * around,
ch 1, join in 3rd st of ch (80 sps). **Rnd 10:**
Ch 3 (counts as 1 dc), 1 dc in each of the
next 10 sps and in each of the 10 dc, * ch 5,
skip 2 sps, sc in next dc, (ch 4, skip 2 sps,
sc in next dc) 3 times, ch 5, skip 2 sps, 1 dc
in each of the next 11 dc and in each of the
10 sps, rep from * twice, ch 5, skip 2 sps,
sc in next dc, (ch 4, skip 2 sps, sc in next
dc) 3 times, ch 5, join. **Rnd 11:** Ch 1, sc in
same sp, 1 sc in each of the next 20 dc, 2 sc
over next lp, * ch 6, 5 dc popcorn st in next
lp (popcorn st: 5 dc in same sp, drop lp
from hk, insert in 1st dc, pick up lp and draw
through), ch 3, popcorn st in next lp, ch 3,
popcorn st in next lp, ch 6, 2 sc over next lp,
1 sc in each of the next 21 dc, 2 sc over
next lp, rep from * twice ending with ch 6,
popcorn st in next lp, (ch 3, popcorn st in
next lp) twice, ch 6, 2 sc over next lp, do
not join. **Rnd 12:** 1 sc in each of the next 23
sc, * 2 sc over next lp, ch 7, popcorn st in
next lp, ch 3, popcorn st in next lp, ch 7,
2 sc over next lp, 1 sc in each of the next 25
sc, rep from * twice, 2 sc over next lp, ch 7,
popcorn st in next lp, ch 3, popcorn st in
next lp, ch 7, 2 sc over next lp, 1 sc in each of
the next 2 sc. **Rnd 13:** 1 sc in each of the
next 25 sc, * 2 sc over next lp, ch 8, popcorn
st in next lp, ch 8, 2 sc over next lp, 1 sc in
each of the next 29 sc, rep from * twice, 2 sc
over next lp, ch 8, popcorn st in next lp,

ch 8, 2 sc over next lp, 1 sc in each of the next 4 sc. **Rnd 14:** 1 sc in each of the next 27 sc, * 2 sc over next lp, ch 7, dc in top of next popcorn st, ch 3, dc in same sp, ch 7, 2 sc over next lp, 1 sc in each of the next 33 sc, rep from * twice, 2 sc over next lp, ch 7, dc in top of next popcorn st, ch 3, dc in same sp, ch 7, 2 sc over next lp, 1 sc in each of the next 6 sc, sl st in next sc and fasten off. Sew motifs together through tops of the sc's and arrange them 12 motifs in width by 15 in length.

Joining Motif: Ch 4, join with a sl st to form a ring. Ch 1, work 8 sc in center of ring, join. **Rnd 2:** Ch 3, join to corner of 1 large motif, ch 3, skip 1 sc of joining motif, sc in next sc, * ch 3, join to corner of next large motif, ch 3, skip 1 sc of joining motif, sc in next st, rep from * twice, join and fasten off.

Edging: Attach thread in corner lp of one motif, ch 5, dc in same sp, * ch 2, skip 1 st, dc in next st, rep from * across motif to next corner of same motif, ch 2, work 1 dc, ch 2 and 1 dc in corner lp, then 1 dc, ch 2 and 1 dc in corner lp of the next motif, rep from 1st * around, always working 1 dc, ch 2 and 1 dc in each corner lp. Ch 2 and join in 3rd st of starting ch. **Rnd 2:** Sl st into corner st, ch 5, 2 tr c cluster st in same sp, * ch 5, skip 1 sp, sl st in next sp, ch 5, 2 tr c cluster st in same sp, rep from * around, ch 5 at end of rnd, join and fasten off. Starch piece lightly and press.

MOUNTAIN MEADOW
As shown on page 109

Design and directions courtesy of Coats & Clark, Inc.

Each strip measures 6 x 91 inches. Cloth measures 72 x 92 inches.

MATERIALS: Clark's Big Ball Mercerized Crochet, Art. B.34, size 30: 13 balls or Art. B.345, size 30: 8 balls. Steel crochet hook No. 10.

GAUGE: 5 sps = 1 inch; 5 rows = 1 inch

Strips: (Make 4): Starting at A on chart, ch 92 to measure 6½ inches. **Row 1:** Dc in 8th ch from hk, ch 2, skip 2 ch, dc in next ch (2 sps made). Work 27 more sps, ch 5, turn. **Row 2:** Skip 1st dc, dc in next dc (sp made over sp), 2 dc in next sp, dc in next dc (bl made over sp). Work 26 more bls, ch 2, skip 2 ch, dc in next ch, ch 5, turn. **Row 3:** Sp over sp, dc in each of the next 3 dc (bl made over bl), ch 2, skip 2 dc, dc in next dc (sp made over bl), 3 more sps, 1 bl, 1 sp, 1 bl, 18 sps, 1 bl, 1 sp, ch 5, turn. **Row 4:** 1 sp, 1 bl, 4 sps, 1 bl, 13 sps, 1 bl, 1 sp, 1 bl, 4 sps, 1 bl, 1 sp, ch 5, turn. Follow chart now to C, then rep from B to C 11 more times, then from C to D once. Fasten off.

Cut 5 linen strips, each to measure 10 x 91½ inches, and make a rolled hem around all edges. Finished strip should measure 9½ x 91 inches. Alternate a linen and lace strip and sew neatly in place.

Edging: Attach thread to edge and work sc closely around all edges, keeping work flat and working a picot every ½ inch.

To Make a Picot: Ch 5, then work a sl st in the last sc. Block piece to measurements.

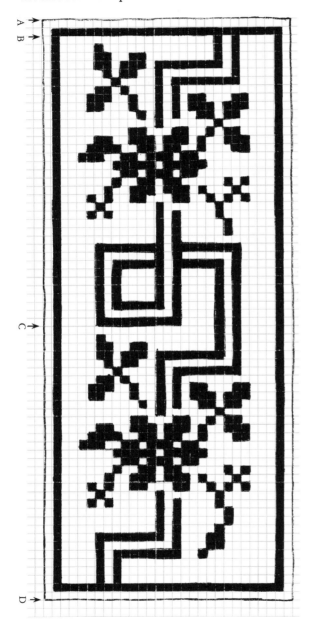

PURITAN

As shown on page 110

Design and directions courtesy of American Thread Company

Each motif measures 5 inches. Bedspread measures approximately 60 x 90 inches without fringe.

MATERIALS: Puritan Mercerized Crochet Cotton: 56 250-yard balls. Steel crochet hook No. 7.

Motifs (Make 216): Ch 6, join with a sl st to form a ring. **Rnd 2:** Ch 6, dc in center of ring, * ch 3, dc in same ring, rep from * 5 times, ch 3, join in 3rd st of ch. **Rnd 3:** Ch 1, 2 sc in 1st lp, then work petal as follows: * Ch 14, dc in 6th st from hk, (ch 2, skip 2 sts of ch, dc in next st) twice, ch 1, turn, 1 sc in dc, 2 sc in next lp, 1 sc in next dc, 2 sc in next lp, 1 sc in next dc, 1 sc in each of the next 2 sts of ch, 3 sc in next st of ch, 1 sc in each of the next 2 sts of ch, 1 sc in base of next dc, 2 sc in next lp, 1 sc in base of next dc, 2 sc in next lp, 1 sc in base of last dc, ch 1, turn, 1 sc in each of the next 10 sc, then working in back lp of sts only for remainder of petal, work 3 sc in next st, 1 sc in each of the next 10 sc, ch 1, turn, 1 sc in each of the next 11 sc, 3 sc in next st, 1 sc in each of the next 11 sc, * ch 1, turn, 1 sc in each of the next 12 sc, 3 sc in next st, 1 sc in each of the next 12 sc. With right side of work toward you, slip lp off hk now, fold petal through center lengthwise, insert hk in 1st st of same sc row of petal, pick up and draw lp through, sl st across lower edge of petal and, working through both thicknesses, sl st in the 2 remaining chs of stem, flatten petal, work 2 sc over remainder of 1st sp, ch 5, sl st in 5th st from hk for picot, 2 sc in next sp, then rep from * once, ch 1, turn. Work 1 sc now in each of the 1st 3 sc, working in back lp of sts only, slip lp off hk, insert hk in back lp of corresponding st of previous petal, draw lp through to join work, 1 sc in each of the next 3 sc, join to corresponding st of previous petal, 1 sc in each of the next 6 sc, 3 sc in next st, 1 sc in each of the next 12 sc, complete petal in same manner as previous petal. Continue in this way until there are 8 petals, then joining the last petal to the 1st petal, sl st in 2 sts of stem, work 2 sc in same sp, picot, join and fasten off. **Rnd 4:** Join thread in point of petal, ch 6, dc in same sp, (ch 2, skip 1 st, dc in next st) twice, ch 2, skip 1 st, tr c in next st, skip 1st free st on next petal, tr c in next st, (ch 2, skip 1 st, dc in next st) twice, ch 2, skip 1 st, dc in point of petal, ch 3, dc in same sp, rep from * around, ch 2, join in 3rd st of ch. **Rnd 5:** Ch 1, * 3 sc in sp (1 sc in next dc, 2 sc in next sp) 3 times, skip next 2 tr c, 2 sc in each of the next 3 sps, 1 sc in each of the next 3 dc, rep from * around. **Rnd 6:** * Ch 5, skip 3 sc, 1 sc in each of the next 7 sc, ch 3, skip 4 sc, 1 sc in each of the next 17 sc, ch 3, skip 4 sc, 1 sc in each of the next 7 sc, rep from * around. **Rnd 7:** Sl st in lp, ch 6, tr c in same lp, (ch 1, tr c in same lp) 5 times, * ch 3, skip 1 sc, 1 sc in each of the next 5 sc, ch 4, skip 1 sc of next group of sc, 1 sc in each of the next 15 sc, ch 4, skip 1 sc of next

group of sc, 1 sc in each of the next 5 sc, ch 3, 1 tr c in next lp, (ch 1, tr c in same lp) 6 times, rep from * around, ch 3, join in 5th st of ch. **Rnd 8:** Sc in next lp, (ch 3, sc in next lp) 6 times, * ch 3, skip 1 sc, 1 sc in each of the next 3 sc, ch 3, dc in next lp, ch 3, skip 1 sc, 1 sc in each of the next 13 sc, ch 3, dc in next lp, ch 3, skip 1 sc, 1 sc in each of the next 3 sc, (ch 3, sc in next lp) 8 times, rep from * around, completing the lps at corner. **Rnd 9:** Sl st in next lp, (ch 2, sc in next lp) twice, ch 3, sc in same lp (corner), (ch 2, sc in next lp) 4 times, (ch 2, dc in next lp) twice, ch 2, skip 2 sc, 1 sc in each of the next 9 sc, (ch 2, dc in next lp) twice, (ch 2, sc in next lp) 5 times, ch 3, sc in same lp (ch 2, sc in next lp) 4 times, continue around in same manner. **Rnd 10:** Ch 1, 2 sc in each of the next 2 lps, 5 sc in corner lp, 2 sc in each of the next 4 lps, 3 sc in each of the next 3 lps, skip 1 sc, 1 sc in each of the next 7 sc, continue around in same manner. **Rnd 11:** Working in back lp of sts only work 1 sc in each sc working 3 sc in each corner. Join and fasten off. Work 215 more motifs in the same manner. Sew motifs together with an overcast st, arranging them 12 motifs in width by 18 in length.

Edging: Attach thread to the corner of the spread and working across what will become the top edge, ch 4, dc in same sp, * ch 1, skip 1 st, dc in next st, rep from * around working 1 dc, ch 1, and 1 dc in center st at each corner, join. **Rnd 2:** * Ch 3, work 2 dc in same sp, skip 1 sp, sl st in next sp, ch 3, work 2 dc in same sp, skip 1 dc and 1 sp, sl st in next dc, rep from * across top edge only, join and fasten off.

Fringe: Cut several strands of yarn, each to measure 14 inches. Using 14 strands, double them in half and loop them through every other space along the 3 sides of the spread, then * take half of one group of fringe and half of the next group and knot them together about ½ inch below the 1st row of knots. Repeat from * around and trim fringe ends evenly. Starch lightly and press.

MOSAIC ROSE
As shown on page 110

Design and directions courtesy of Coats & Clark, Inc.

Single-size spread measures 39 x 96 inches with side drop of 10 inches. Double-size spread measures 52 x 96 inches with side drop of 10 inches.

MATERIALS: Clark's Big Ball Mercerized Crochet, Art. B.34, size 20: 42 balls for single-size spread, 51 balls for double-size spread, or Art. B.345, size 20: 28 balls for single-size spread, 34 balls for double-size spread. Steel crochet hook No. 11.

GAUGE: 5 sps or 5 bls = 1 inch. 5 rows = 1 inch

Strips (Make 3 for single-size spread and 4 for double-size spread): Starting at narrow edge, make a chain 16 inches long having 15 ch to 1 inch. **Row 1:** Starting at A on chart, work a dc in 4th ch from hk (starting bl made), ch 2, skip 2 ch, dc in next ch (sp made), dc in each of next 3 ch (bl made), work 5 more bls, 3 sps, 43 bls, 3 sps, 6 bls, 1 sp, then work a dc in the next ch (ending

bl made). Cut off any remaining ch, ch 3, turn. **Row 2:** Skip 1st dc, dc in next dc (starting bl over ending bl made), ch 2, dc in next dc (sp over sp made) dc in back lp of each of the next 3 dc (bl over bl made) then working in back lp only of each dc, make 2 more bls, then ch 2, skip 2 dc, dc through both lps of next dc (sp over bl made) make 2 bls as before, 2 dc in next sp, dc through both lps of next dc (bl over sp made). Working bls over bls now as before, make 1 sp, 3 bls, 2 sps, 5 bls, 25 sps, 5 bls, 2 sps (3 bls, 1 sp) 3 times, then dc in next dc and in top of turning ch (ending bl over starting bl made), ch 3, turn.

Note: From this point on, when making a bl over bl, always work in the back lp only of each dc. **Next 58 Rows:** Following chart, work from B to C once, then from A to C 7 times. Fasten off at end of last row. Sew strips neatly together. Block spread to measurements.

Border: Starting at narrow edge, make a chain 9 inches long, having 15 ch to 1 inch. **Row 1:** Starting at A on Chart 2 and working as for 1st row of strip, work 1 starting bl, 5 sps, 7 bls, 11 sps, 1 bl, 1 sp, 1 bl, 4 sps, 1 bl, 1 sp, 1 bl, 2 sps, 1 bl, dc in each of the next 3 ch (end bl made at shaped edge). Cut off any remaining chain, ch 8, turn. **Row 2:** Dc in 4th ch from hk and in each of the next 4 ch, dc in next dc (2 bls increased at beg of row), then working bls over bls as on strips, work 1 bl, 4 sps, 1 bl, 6 sps, 2 bls, 9 sps, 2 bls, 2 sps, 1 bl, 1 sp, 1 bl, 2 sps, 2 bls, 3 sps, and

1 ending bl as on strips, ch 3, turn. **Next 12 Rows:** Following Chart 2, work from B to C. **Next Row:** Follow 15th row to within last 2 bls of previous row but do not work over last 2 bls (2 bls decreased). Ch 3, turn. Continue to follow chart to D. Rep from A to D 25 times more for single spread or 27 times more for double spread.

Press border. Leaving top edge of bedspread free, pin straight edge of border to side edges and lower edge of bedspread, gathering the excess length at each corner of lower edge. Sew edges neatly together. Starch lightly and press.

← C

← B
← A

■ BLOCK   □ SPACE

D

15th
ROW

C

B
A

PINEAPPLE PARFAIT

As shown on page 112

Design and directions courtesy of Coats & Clark, Inc.

Each motif measures 8½ inches square. Afghan measures 43 x 60 inches, excluding borders.

MATERIALS: Coats & Clark Red Heart 2-ply Wintuk Sport Yarn: 22 ounces. Steel crochet hook No. 0.

First Motif: Starting at center, ch 8, join with a sl st to form a ring. **Rnd 1:** Ch 4, work 27 tr c in center of ring, join with a sl st to top of ch-4. **Rnd 2:** Ch 5, skip joining, * tr c in next tr c, ch 1, rep from * around, join to 4th ch of ch-5. **Rnd 3:** In 1st sp, work a sl st, ch 1, and sc, then * ch 3, sc in next sp, rep from * around, ending with ch 1, and a hdc in 1st sc to form the last lp—28 lps. **Rnd 4:** Ch 3, dc in same lp, * ch 5, skip next 2 lps, 9 dc in next lp, ch 5, skip next 2 lps and holding back on hk the last lp of each dc, work 2 dc in next lp, yarn over and draw through all 3 lps on hk (cluster made), ch 3, cluster in next lp, rep from * around, ending with ch 3. Join to 1st dc. **Rnd 5:** Ch 3, dc in joining, 3 ch 5, (tr c in next tr c, ch 1) 8 times, tr c in next tr c, (ch 5, cluster in tip of next cluster) twice, rep from * around, ending with ch 5. Join as before. **Rnd 6:** Ch 3, dc in joining, * ch 5, (sc in next ch-1 sp, ch 3) 7 times, sc in next sp, ch 5, cluster in tip of next cluster, ch 7 for corner lp, cluster in tip of next cluster, rep from * around, ending with ch 7, join. **Rnd 7:** Ch 3, dc in joining, * ch 5, (sc in next ch-3 lp, ch 3) 6 times, sc in next lp, ch 5, cluster in tip of next cluster, ch 5, in next corner lp work 2 dc, ch 5 and 2 dc, ch 5, cluster in tip of next cluster, rep from * around, ending with 2 dc, ch 5, and 2 dc in last lp, then ch 5, join. **Rnd 8:** Ch 3, dc in joining, * ch 5, (sc in next ch-3 lp, ch 3) 5 times, sc in next lp, ch 5, cluster in tip of next cluster, ch 5, dc in each of the next 2 dc, in next ch-5 lp work 2 dc, ch 5 and 2 dc, dc in each of the next 2 dc, ch 5, cluster in tip of next cluster, rep from * around, ending

with ch 5, join. **Rnd 9:** Ch 3, dc in joining, * ch 5, (sc in next ch-3 lp, ch 3) 4 times, sc in next lp, ch 5, cluster in tip of next cluster, ch 5, dc in each of the next 4 dc, in next ch-5 lp work 2 dc, ch 5 and 2 dc, dc in each of the next 4 dc, ch 5, cluster in tip of next cluster, rep from * around, ending with dc in each of the next 4 dc, ch 5, join. **Rnd 10:** Ch 3, dc in joining, * ch 9, holding back on hk the last lp of each tr c, work 1 tr c in each of the next 4 ch-3 lps, yarn over and draw through all 5 lps on hk, ch 9, cluster in tip of next cluster, ch 5, dc in each of the next 4 dc, ch 5, skip next 2 dc, in next ch-5 lp work 2 dc, ch 7 and 2 dc, ch 5, skip next 2 dc, dc in each of the next 4 dc, ch 5, cluster in tip of the next cluster, rep from * around, ending with a dc in each of the last 4 dc, ch 5, join. **Rnd 11:** Ch 1, * sc in next lp, ch 6, sc in 4th ch from hk, ch 2, sc in same lp (picot lp made), ch 6, sc in 4th ch from hk, ch 2, rep from * around—56 picot lps. Join with a sl st to 1st sc and fasten off.

Second Motif: Work as for 1st motif until the 10th rnd has been completed. **Rnd 11:** Ch 1, (work a picot lp in the next lp, ch 6, sc in 4th ch from hk, ch 2) 4 times, then join 2 sides of 2 motifs as follows: sc in next corner lp, ch 4, sl st in any corner picot lp on 1st motif, * ch 1, sc in 3rd ch of ch-4 on 2nd motif, ch 2, sc in same lp on 2nd motif, ch 4, sl st in next picot lp on 1st motif, ch 1, sc in 3rd ch of ch-4 on 2nd motif, ch 2, sc in next lp on 2nd motif, ch 4, sl st in next picot lp on 1st motif, rep from * across to within next corner picot lp, ch 1, sc in 3rd ch of ch-4 on 2nd motif, ch 2, sc in corner lp on 2nd motif, ch 4, sl st in next corner picot lp on 1st motif, ch 1, sc in 3rd ch of ch-4 on 2nd motif, sc in same corner lp on 2nd motif (2 motifs are joined), ch 6, sc in 4th ch from hk, ch 2, then starting at * on 11th rnd of 1st motif, complete as for 1st motif and fasten off.

Make 5 rows of 7 motifs, joining motifs as 2nd motif was joined to 1st motif (where 4 corners meet, join corners to previous joinings). Block to measurements.

Border: With right side of work facing, attach yarn to any corner picot lp, ch 1, sc in same place where yarn was attached, ch 6, sc in 4th ch from hk, ch 2, sc in same lp, * (ch 6, sc in 4th ch from hk, ch 2, sc in next picot lp) 13 times, ch 6, sc in 4th ch from hk, ch 2, sc in joining between motifs, rep from * around, working a picot lp in each of the 3 remaining corner picot lps in same manner as on first corner. Fasten off.

INTERMEZZO
As shown on page 116

Design and directions courtesy of Bernhard Ulmann Company

Each strip is approximately 7½ inches wide. Shawl measures 30 inches wide x 75 inches long, including fringe.

MATERIALS: Bear Brand, Fleisher's, or Botany Spectator: 10 2-ounce balls. Aluminum crochet hook No. F.

GAUGE: 2 rows = 1 inch

Strips (Make 4): **Row 1:** Ch 10, work 1 dc in 8th ch from hk to form 1st ring, ch 5, join with a sl st in 1st ch of ch 10 to form the 2nd ring. **Row 2:** Ch 3, turn, work 10 dc in each ring—21 dc (ch 3 at beg of row counts as 1 dc). **Row 3:** Ch 3, turn, skip 2nd dc, 1 dc in next dc, * ch 1, skip next dc, 1 dc in next dc, rep from * across and end ch 1, 1 dc in top of ch 3—10 sps. **Row 4:** Ch 3, turn, work 3 dc in 1st ch-1 sp, * skip next dc, 3 dc in next ch-1 sp, rep from * across and end 3 dc in last sp—31 dc. **Row 5:** Ch 4, turn, skip 2nd dc, work 1 dc in next dc, * ch 2, skip next dc, 1 dc in next dc, rep from * across and end ch 1, 1 dc in top of ch 3—15 sps and the end of the 1st fan. **Row 6:** Ch 5, turn, skip 1st ch-2 sp, work 1 dc in the next ch-2 sp, ch 5, skip next ch-2 sp, 1 dc in the next dc (start of 2nd fan) sl st in each of the next 2 ch, sl st in next dc. **Row 7:** Ch 1, turn, work 10 dc in each of the 2 rings—20 dc. **Row 8:** Ch 3, turn, skip 2nd dc, work 1 dc in the next dc, * ch 1, skip next dc, 1 dc in next dc, rep from * across and end ch 1, 1 dc in turning ch-1, ch 1, sl st in next free dc of 1st fan, sl st in each of next 2 ch and in next dc of 1st fan—11 sps. **Row 9:** Ch 1, turn, work 3 dc in each of the 1st 5 sps, 4 dc in 6th sp, 3 dc in each of the last 5 sps—34 dc. **Row 10:** Ch 4, turn, skip 2nd dc, work 1 dc in the next dc, * ch 2, skip next dc, 1 dc in next dc, rep from * across and end last repeat with ch 2, 1 dc in turning ch-1, ch 2, sl st in next free dc of 1st fan—18 sps. Mark start of last row. **Row 11:** Ch 5, turn, skip 1st ch-2 sp, work 1 dc in next ch-2 sp of last fan, ch 5, skip next ch-2 sp, sl st in next dc (start of next fan), sl st in each of next 2 ch and next dc of last fan. **Row 12:** Ch 1, turn, work 10 dc in each of 2 rings, sl st in next free dc of adjacent fan, sl st in each of the next 2 ch and next dc of the same fan—20 dc. **Row 13:** Ch 1, turn, skip 1st dc, work 1 dc in next dc, * ch 1, skip next dc, 1 dc in next dc, rep from * 9 times, ch 1, sl st in next free dc of adjacent fan, sl st in each of the next 2 ch and next dc—11 sps. **Row 14:** Ch 1, turn, work 3 dc in each of the 1st 5 ch-1 sps, 4 dc in the 6th ch-1 sp, 3 dc in each of the last 5 ch-1 sps, sl st in the next free dc of the adjacent fan, sl st in each of the next 2 ch and the next dc—34 dc. **Row 15:** Ch 2, turn, skip 1st dc, work 1 dc in the next dc, * ch 2, skip next dc, 1 dc in the next dc, rep from * 15 times, ch 2, sl st in the next free dc of the adjacent fan—18 sps. Repeat from Row 11 30 times more—33 fans have been made and the piece measures approximately 65 inches. Fasten off. Mark the end of the last row.

Finishing: With right side of strip facing and working opposite 1st fan of one strip, join yarn with a sl st to the top of the starting ch of Row 2, work 8 dc in each ring of the 1st fan, join with a sl st to the last dc of Row 2, then work 2 sl sts in the starting ch of Row 3, and 1 sl st in top of same ch. **Row 2:** Ch 1, turn, skip 1st dc, 1 dc in next dc, * ch 1, skip next dc, 1 dc in next dc, rep from * across and end ch 1, sl st in top of last dc of Row 3 of 1st fan, sl st in each of 3 ch of beginning ch of Row 4 of 1st fan—9 sps.

Row 3: Ch 1, turn, work 3 dc in each of the 1st 4 ch-1 sps, 4 dc in the 5th ch-1 sp, 3 dc in each of the last 4 ch-1 sps, join with a sl st in top of the last dc of Row 4 of 1st fan, sl st in each of the 1st 3 ch of the starting ch of Row 5 of the 1st fan—28 dc. **Row 4:** Ch 2, turn, skip 1st dc, work 1 dc in next dc, * ch 2, skip next dc, 1 dc in next dc, rep from * across and end ch 2, join with a sl st in top of last dc of Row 5 of 1st fan. **Row 5:** Ch 5, turn, sl st in 1st dc (ring for half fan made) sl st in each of the next 2 ch, and in the next dc of the last fan. **Row 6:** Ch 1, turn, work 8 dc in center of ring, join with a sl st in top of last dc of Row 7 of 2nd fan, sl st in each of the 3 ch of the starting ch of Row 8. **Row 7:** Ch 1, turn, skip 1st dc, work 1 dc in next dc, * ch 1, skip next dc, 1 dc in next dc, rep from * across and end ch 1, and join with a sl st in top of the next free dc of the last fan, sl st in each of the next 2 ch and the next dc—5 sps. **Row 8:** Ch 1, turn, work 3 dc in each of the 1st 2 ch-1 sps, 4 dc in the 3rd ch-1 sp, 3 dc in each of the last 2 ch-1 sps, join with a sl st in top of the last dc of Row 9 of the 2nd fan, sl st in each of the 1st 3 ch of the starting ch of Row 10. **Row 9:** Ch 2, turn, skip 1st dc, work 1 dc in the next dc, * ch 2, skip next dc, 1 dc in next dc, rep from * across and end ch 2, sl st in the next free dc of the last fan—9 sps. Fasten off.

Place 2 strips on a flat surface with end of strips toward you, having the beginning of the 1st strip to the right and the end of the 2nd strip adjacent to the beginning of the 1st strip on the left. Sew strips together with an overcast st, starting with the marked sts at the beginning of the 1st strip and the end of the 2nd strip and working to the marked sts at the opposite end. Sew the 3rd and 4th strips together in same manner. Place the 3rd and 4th strips to the left of the 1st and 2nd strips. Count 11 sps from the seam of the 1st 2 strips, beginning with the next dc and the 3rd ch of the starting ch of Row 5 of the 1st fan of adjacent strip, then sew in same manner as before to corresponding sts at opposite end of strips.

Fringe: Cut several strands of yarn, each to measure 14 inches. Knot 4-strand fringe in the spaces along each end of the shawl. Trim fringe ends evenly. Block.

NANETTE
As shown on page 118

Design and directions courtesy of William Unger & Co., Inc.

Each motif attached measures 4 inches. Shawl measures approximately 36 x 60 inches, measuring through the center.

MATERIALS: Unger's Nanette: 11 50-gram balls. Aluminum crochet hook No. G.

First Motif: Ch 5, join with a sl st to form a ring. **Rnd 1:** Ch 1, work 8 sc in center of ring, join with a sl st. **Rnd 2:** Ch 1, sc in same sp, * ch 3, sc in next st, rep from * 6 times more and end with ch 3, join with a sl st to 1st sc—8 ch and 3 sps made. **Rnd 3:** Work 1 sc, 3 dc and 1 sc under each ch-3 lp (8 petals), join with a sl st. **Rnd 4:** * Ch 3, keeping lps to back of petal, sc through the back of the next sc between 2 petals of the previous rnd, rep from * around—8 ch lps made, join with a sl st. **Rnd 5:** Rep Rnd 3. **Rnd 6:** * (Ch 5, sl st in 3rd ch from hk for picot) twice, ch 3, sc in same sp as beginning of 1st ch-5 (corner), (ch 5, sl st in 3rd ch from hk, ch 3, sc in next sp between 2 petals) twice, rep from * 3 times (4 corners with 2 picot lps between each corner made).

Second Motif: Rep Rnds 1 through 5 as for 1st motif. **Rnd 6:** *Joining Rnd:* Ch 5, sl st in 3rd ch from hk (picot), ch 2, hold 2nd motif back to back to 1st motif, insert hk through 2nd picot of the 1st corner of the 1st motif and work 1 sc, ch 3 and 1 sc back to the starting ch on the 2nd motif (joined corner of 2nd motif formed), ch 3, sc in picot of the 1st picot lp of the 1st motif, ch 3, sc in sp between the next 2 petals of the 2nd motif, ch 3, sc in the picot of the next picot lp of the 1st motif, ch 3, sc in the sp between the next 2 petals of the 2nd motif, ch 3, sc through the 1st picot of the 2nd corner of the 1st motif, ch 5, sl st in 3rd ch from hk for picot, ch 3, sc in same sp as starting ch at corner of 2nd motif, * (ch 5, sl st in 3rd ch from hk, ch 3, sc in the next sp between 2 petals) twice, (ch 5, sl st in the 3rd ch from hk for picot), twice, ch 3, sc in sp of starting ch-5 (corner), rep from * once more, ch 5, sl st in 3rd ch from hk, ch 3, sc in next sp between 2 petals, ch 5, sl st in 3rd ch from hk, ch 3, join with a sl st to the 1st st. Fasten off.

Third Motif: Rep Rnds 1 through 5 as for

1st motif. **Rnd 6:** *Joining Rnd:* This motif is joined to the 1st motif with the 2nd motif to the left of the 1st motif. Ch 5, sl st in 3rd ch from hk for picot, ch 2, then holding 3rd motif back to back to 1st motif, (2nd motif to left of 1st motif), insert hk through the 2nd picot of the corner of the 1st motif and work a sc, ch 3, and 1 sc back to the starting ch on 3rd motif (corner joining), (ch 3, sc in picot of next picot lp on 1st motif, ch 3, sc in sp between 2 petals on 3rd motif) twice, ch 3, sc through 1st picot of the corner of the 1st motif, ch 5, sl st in 3rd ch from hk for picot, ch 3, sc back in same sp as beginning of corner on 3rd motif, * (ch 5, sl st in 3rd ch from hk for picot, ch 3, sc in next sp between 2 petals on 3rd motif) twice, (ch 5, sl st in 3rd ch from hk for picot) twice, ch 3, sc in same sp at start of 1st ch-5 (corner of 3rd motif), rep from * once more, ch 5, sl st in 3rd ch from hk for picot, ch 3, sc in next sp between next 2 petals on 3rd motif, ch 5, sl st in 3rd ch from hk for picot, ch 3, join with a sl st in next sp between petals. Fasten off.

Fourth Motif: Rep Rnds 1 through 5 as for 3rd motif. **Rnd 6:** *Joining Rnd:* This motif is now joined to the 2nd and 3rd motifs. Ch 5, sl st in 3rd ch from hk for picot, ch 2, hold 4th motif back to back to 3rd motif, with 1st motif above the 3rd motif, sc in 2nd picot of the corner of the 3rd motif, ch 3, sc back to starting ch on 4th motif (corner joining), (ch 3, sc in picot of the next picot lp on the 3rd motif, ch 3, sc in the next sp between 2 petals on the 4th motif) twice,

ch 3, sc through the remaining picot on the corner of the 3rd motif, ch 2, sc through the remaining picot on the corner of the 2nd motif, ch 3, sc back in corner on the 4th motif (all 4 motifs are joined at this point), then holding back to back to 2nd motif (ch 3, sc in picot of next picot lp of the 2nd motif, ch 3, sc in next sp between 2 petals on the 4th motif) twice, ch 3, sc in the 1st picot of corner on the 2nd motif, ch 5, sl st in 3rd ch from hk for picot, ch 3, sc back to corner on the 4th motif (3rd corner of 4th motif joined), * (ch 5, sl st in 3rd ch from hk for picot, ch 3, sc in next sp between 2 petals on 4th motif) twice, * (ch 5, sl st in 3rd ch from hk for picot) twice, ch 3, sc in sp at corner of the 4th motif (4th corner of 4th motif) then rep between *'s once and join to beg of rnd with a sl st. Fasten off. 4 motifs have now been joined to form a square. Continue to join motifs in this manner into squares until there are 6 motifs across by 6 motifs high (36 motifs). See chart below and turn square as shown on chart so that it

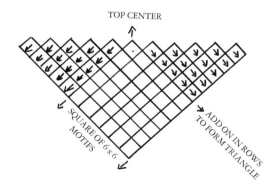

forms a diamond shape. Mark top motif of the diamond for center top, then attach motifs on each side, building up a triangle as shown on chart.

Finishing Top Edging: **Row 1:** Attach yarn in 2nd picot on side corner of motif next to the top edge, * ch 3, sc in picot of picot lp, ch 4, sc in picot of next picot lp, ch 4, sc in 1st picot of corner at top edge, work 1 sc between picots of corner, sc in next picot of same corner, ch 4, sc in picot of next picot lp, ch 3, sc in free picot on corner, ch 2, sc in free picot on corner of next motif, rep from * across entire top edge, ending at 1st corner picot of the opposite side edge, ch 1, turn. **Row 2:** Sc in same sp, (ch 1, sc under ch bar, ch 1, sc in next sc) twice, ch 1, sc under ch bar, ch 1, * sc in next sc, 2 sc in next sc (top of corner), sc in next sc, ch 1, sc under ch bar, ch 1, sc in next sc, ch 2, d tr under ch-2 of row below, ch 2, sc in sc above 2nd picot lp (omitting lp at lower edge), ch 1, sc under ch bar, ch 1, rep from * across, ending sc in next sc, 2 sc in next sc (top of corner), (sc in next st, ch 1, sc under ch bar, ch 1) 3 times, sc in the 1st picot of the corner at the side edge. Fasten off.

Fringe: Cut several strands of yarn, each to measure 16". Using 5 strands for each fringe, fold in half and draw loop through the same corner at the side where the top edge was started, then pass all loose ends through the loop and knot. Work a fringe in each picot loop and each corner loop along both side edges of the shawl.

MIA

As shown on page 123

Design and directions courtesy of Reynolds Yarns, Inc.

Slipover has been designed for small size (10–12). Changes for medium (14–16) and large (18–20) are in parentheses.

MATERIALS: Reynolds Classique: 6 (7, 8) balls. Steel crochet hook No. 5.

GAUGE: Tr c and ch 10 = 1 inch

PATTERN STITCH:

Row 1: Ch 6, yarn over hk, draw up a lp in the 6th ch from hk, (yarn over, draw up a lp in the same ch) 3 times, yarn over and through all 9 lps on hk, ch 1 tightly, work 1 sl st in the same ch (upside down cluster made), * ch 15, work an upside down cluster in the 5th ch from hk, rep from * to end.
Row 2: Ch 4, turn, tr c in same ch as 1st cluster, * ch 10, tr c in the same ch as next cluster, rep from * and end ch 10, tr c in same ch as last cluster.
Row 3: Ch 14, turn, skip 1st tr c, yarn over, draw up a lp in the next tr c, (yarn over, draw up a lp in the same tr c) 3 times, yarn over, insert hk from front to back under ch to right of the tr c, draw up a lp, yarn over and through all lps on hk, ch 1 tightly (cluster made), * ch 10, tr c in next tr c, ch 20, turn, sl st in last tr c worked to form a lp, work 2 sc over the ch-10 at the left of the lp, turn, work 25 dc around the ch-20 lp, mark the center dc, then ch 8, work a cluster in the next tr c, rep from * and end ch 10, tr c in last tr c.

Row 4: Ch 14, turn, tr c in top of 1st cluster, * ch 10, tr c in the next tr c, working behind the lp, ch 10, tr c in top of next cluster, rep from * and end ch 10, tr c in 4th ch from end of ch-14 of last row.

Row 5: Ch 14, turn, cluster in tr c above the 1st cluster of 2 rows below, * ch 10, tr c in the next tr c, ch 10, cluster in the next tr c, rep from * and end ch 10, tr c in 4th ch from end of ch-14 of last row.

Row 6: Work same as Row 4.

Row 7: Ch 14, turn, cluster in the tr c above the 1st cluster of 2 rows below, * ch 10, tr c in next tr c, sl st in top of the marked dc of lp, ch 20, turn, sl st in the last tr c worked to form a lp, work 1 sc in each of the next 2 dc to the left of the marked dc of lp (11th and 12th dc), turn, work 25 dc around the ch-20 lp, mark the center dc, work 1 sl st in the dc to the left of the marked dc in lp below, ch 8, cluster in next tr c, rep from * and end ch 10, tr c in 4th ch from end of the ch-14 of last row.

Row 8: Work same as Row 4. Repeat last 4 rows for pattern.

Back: Work Row 1 of pattern until there are 17 (19, 21) upside down clusters. Continue in pattern until there are 22 rows ending with Row 6 of pattern. Piece should now measure approximately 8 inches. Fasten off. *Shape Armholes:* **Row 1:** Skip 1st tr c and 1st ch-10, join yarn in next tr c, ch 14, tr c in next tr c, continue in the pattern and end with a tr c in the last tr c (leave ch-14 for the other armhole). Continue in pattern (omitting cluster at ends of rows) until there are 42 (42, 46) rows from beginning. Armholes should measure approximately 8 (8, 9) inches. **Last Row:** Ch 14, turn, * tr c in back of 1st lp, sl st in top of marked dc, ch 10, cluster in next tr c, ch 10, rep from * ending with a tr c in the 4th ch of ch-14. Fasten off.

Front: Work same as back.

Sleeves: Work pattern Row 1 until there are 13 (13, 15) upside-down clusters, then continue pattern until there are 18 rows. Fasten off.

Top Shaping: **Row 1:** Work same as Row 1 of armholes. Continue in pattern until there are 26 rows. Fasten off. **Next Row:** Join yarn in tr c in back of 1st lp, ch 4, sl st in top of marked dc of lp, ch 10, cluster in next tr c, ch 10, tr c in next tr c (in back of next lp), then continue pattern and end tr c in last tr c in back of last lp, sl st in top of marked dc of lp (1 lp dec at each end). Continue in pattern for 8 rows more. **Last Row:** Work same as last row of armholes. Fasten off.

Finishing: Weave back and front together, matching pattern rows. Weave shoulders together from armhole edges until 2 (2, 3) lps at each side have been joined. Weave sleeve seams. With center of last row of sleeves at shoulder seams and 1st row of armholes matching 1st row of sleeves, weave sleeves to armholes. *Edging:* Starting at right shoulder seam and working from right side, work across the back neck edge as follows: 5 sc under the 1st ch-10, ch 4, (yarn over, draw up a lp in the side of the 5th sc) 5 times, yarn over and through all lps, ch 1 tightly, work 4 sc under the same ch, * 5 sc under next ch-10, ch 4, (yarn over, draw up a lp in side of the 5th sc) 5 times, ch 1 tightly, 4 sc under same ch-10, rep from * around neck edge and join with sl st to 1st sc. Fasten off. Work a crochet edge around the lower edge of the sleeves in the same way.

LACE SQUARES

As shown on page 124

Design and directions courtesy of Emile Bernat & Sons Company

Dress has been designed for size 10. Changes for sizes 12, 14, 16 are in parentheses.

MATERIALS: Bernat Meadowspun: 11 (12, 14, 15) 1-ounce skeins. Steel crochet hook No. 00. Snap fasteners. Lining, if desired.

GAUGE: 4 sts = 1 inch

PATTERN STITCH:

Row 1: 1 sc in 2nd ch from hk, 1 sc in each of the next 2 sts, * ch 7, skip 2 sts, 1 sc in each of the next 7 sts, rep from *, ending with 1 sc in each of the last 4 sts, ch 1, turn.
Row 2: Skip 1 sc, 1 sc in each of the next 2 sc, * ch 3, 1 sc in next ch-7 sp, ch 3, skip 1 sc, 1 sc in each of the next 5 sc, rep from * ending skip 1 sc, 1 sc in each of the last 2 sc, ch 1, turn.
Row 3: 1 sc in 2nd sc, * ch 3, 1 sc in ch-3 sp, 1 sc in the next sc, 1 sc in the next ch-3 sp, ch 3, skip 1 sc, 1 sc in each of the next 3 sc, rep from * ending with 1 sc in each of the last 2 sc, turn.
Row 4: Ch 4, * 1 sc in the next ch-3 sp, 1 sc in each of the next 3 sc, 1 sc in the next ch-3 sp, ch 3, skip 1 sc, 1 sc in the next sc, ch 3, rep from * ending ch 3 and 1 sc in last sc, turn.
Row 5: Ch 3, * 1 sc in ch-3 sp, 1 sc in each of the next 5 sc, 1 sc in the next ch-3 sp, ch 7, rep from * ending with ch 3, and 1 sc in the last ch sp, turn.
Row 6: Ch 4, * skip 1 sc, 1 sc in each of the next 5 sc, ch 3, 1 sc in the next ch-7 sp, ch 3, rep from * ending ch 3 and 1 sc in the last ch sp, turn.
Row 7: Ch 1, 1 sc in the next sc, 1 sc in the next ch-3 sp, * ch 3, skip 1 sc, 1 sc in each of the next 3 sc, ch 3, 1 sc in the next ch-3 sp, 1 sc in the next sc, 1 sc in the next ch-3 sp, rep from * ending with ch 3, 1 sc in the next ch-3 sp, 1 sc in the last ch sp, turn.
Row 8: Ch 1, 1 sc in each of the next 2 sts, * ch 3, skip next st, 1 sc in the next sc, ch 3, 1 sc in the next ch-3 sp, 1 sc in each of the next 3 sc, 1 sc in the next ch-3 sp, rep from * ending 1 sc in the next ch-3 sp, 1 sc in each of the last 2 sts, ch 1, turn.
Row 9: 1 sc in each of the next 3 sc, * ch 7, 1 sc in the 2nd ch-3 sp, 1 sc in each of the

next 5 sc, 1 sc in the next ch-3 sp, rep from * ending ch 7, 1 sc in the 2nd ch-3 sp, 1 sc in each of the last 3 sc, ch 1, turn.

Repeat Rows 2 through 9 for pattern stitch.

Note: This dress has been planned for a 29 (29, 29½, 29½)-inch finished length to armhole, including 2½ inches for stretching. If you wish your dress to be longer or shorter, work more or fewer inches before placing your armhole marker.

Back: Ch 73 (73, 82, 82) sts loosely to measure 17½ (17½, 19, 19) inches. Work even in pattern st on 72 (72, 81, 81) sts until entire piece measures 26½ (26½, 27, 27) inches. Put a marker at each end of work to mark start of armholes and work even in pattern st until piece measures 7¼ (7½, 7¾, 8) inches above armhole markers, ending at arm edge with Row 4, turn. *Shape Right Shoulder and Neck:* Ch 3, 1 sc in next ch-3 sp, 1 sc in each of the next 5 sc, 1 sc in the next ch-3 sp, ch 7, 1 sc in the next ch-3 sp, 1 sc in each of the next 5 sc, 1 sc in the next ch-3 sp, ch 7, 1 sc in the next ch-3 sp, 1 sc in each of the next 3 (3, 5, 5) sts, turn. Working now in pattern as established, dec 1 st at neck edge every row 3 times. Fasten off. *Shape Left Shoulder:* Join yarn at arm edge and work in same manner as right shoulder back, reversing all shaping.

Front: Ch 73 (82, 82, 91) sts loosely to measure 17½ (19, 19, 20½) inches. Work to correspond to back.

Neckband: Ch 9 sts loosely to measure 2 inches. **Row 1:** Work 1 sc in 2nd ch from hk, 1 sc in each remaining st of ch, ch 1, turn—8 sts. **Row 2:** 1 sc in each sc, ch 1, turn. **Rows 3, 4, 5, 6, 7, 8:** Rep Row 2. **Row 9:** *Short Rows:* Work 1 sc in each of the 1st 5 sc, 1 sl st in next st, turn. **Row 10:** Skip the sl st, work 1 sc in each of the next 5 sc, ch 1, turn. **Row 11:** Work 1 sc in each of the 1st 5 sc, 1 sc in the sl st, 1 sc in each of the last 2 sts, ch 1, turn—8 sts. Repeat Rows 2 through 11 until neckband is desired length. Fasten off.

Finishing: Using steam iron, press on wrong side only, stretching 2½ inches in length below markers. If lining is desired, cut before seaming. With right side of work facing you, work 1 row of sl st on side edges to underarm markers. Sew side and shoulder seams. Starting at center back, sew neckband to neck edge, easing in any extra fullness. *Edging:* With right side of work facing you and working from left to right along outer edge of neckband, * ch 1, skip 1 st, work 1 hdc in next st, rep from * around outer edge. Fasten off. With right side facing you work 1 row sc around armholes, ch 1, do not turn. Working from left to right now, * ch 1, skip 1 st, work 1 hdc in next st, rep from * around. Fasten off. Line, if desired. Sew on snap fasteners.

EIGHT

Hairpin Lace Directions

HOW TO MAKE HAIRPIN LACE

| STEP 1 | STEP 2 | STEP 3 | STEP 4 |

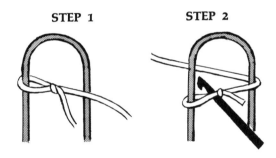 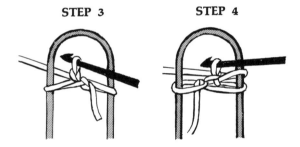

Step 1. Tie a slip loop ½ the width of the loom, remove the bar, place the left prong into the loop, replace bar, then tie a knot at the short end to mark the start of your work.

Step 2. Wind yarn around the right prong of the loom and across the back, then insert crochet hook between the 2 strands of the loop to the left of the center of the loom, placing your hook under the front strand.

Step 3. Place the yarn that is across the back over the hook and draw it through the loop, then reach again for the yarn, place it over the hook and draw it once more through the loop on the hook.

Step 4. Remove the hook from the stitch and reinsert it into the same stitch from the back. Turn the loom toward you now from right to left, thus making a new loop of yarn around the back of the loom.

STEP 5

Step 5. Insert hook between the 2 strands of the loop to the left of the center, placing it under the front strand, then place the yarn that is across the back over the hook, draw it through, then reach again for the yarn and draw it through both loops on hook (single crochet made).

Repeat Steps 2 through 5 for desired length or until the loom has become filled, omitting the winding of the yarn around the right prong in repeating Step 2 since this has been automatically done by the turning of the loom. When the loom has become filled, remove the bar, slide all but the last 4 loops off the loom, replace the bar and continue working as before for the desired length.

For ease in counting the number of loops being worked, either mark every 25th loop on each side of the strip or use stitch count markers on the prongs of the loom.

Abbreviations

bl	block
ch	chain
d tr	double treble
dc	double crochet
dec	decrease
hdc	half double crochet
hk	hook
inc	increase
lp(s)	loop(s)
rep	repeat
rnd	round
sc	single crochet
sl st	slip stitch
sp(s)	space(s)
st(s)	stitch(es)
tr c	treble crochet
*****	indicates that directions following are to be repeated as necessary

MALTESE

As shown on page 105

Design and directions courtesy of Coats & Clark, Inc.

Doily measures 14 inches in diameter.

MATERIALS: Clark's Big Ball Mercerized Crochet Art. B.34: size 10: 1 ball for the Hairpin Lace, size 30: 1 ball for remainder of doily. Steel crochet hook No. 8 for hairpin lace, and No. 10 for remainder of work. Adjustable hairpin loom.

First Hairpin Lace Strip: Adjusting loom to 1 inch, make a strip of hairpin lace having 36 lps on each side of strip. Fasten off, leaving an 8-inch length for sewing.

Keeping all lps twisted throughout and starting at center, attach thread to the 1st lp of hairpin lace strip. **Rnd 1:** Insert hk through the 1st 3 lps and complete an sc, (sc through next 3 lps) 11 times, join with a sl st to the 1st sc. Fasten off. With the

8-inch length, sew ends together at center of strip. **Rnd 2:** Working along opposite side of same strip, attach thread to any lp, ch 1, sc in same place, * ch 3, sc in next lp, rep from * around, ending with ch 3 and join to 1st sc—36 lps. **Rnd 3:** Ch 3, work 4 dc in 1st lp, * dc in next sc, 4 dc in next lp, rep from * around and join to top of ch-3—180 dc, counting the starting ch-3 as 1 dc. **Rnd 4:** Ch 1, sc in joining, * ch 3, skip next 3 dc, sc in next dc, rep from * around, ending with ch 3 and join to 1st sc—45 lps. **Rnd 5:** (Right Side): Ch 1, * in next lp work sc, hdc and 2 dc. Mark the 1st sc made, then work (4 dc in next lp) 7 times, in the next lp work 2 dc, hdc and sc, rep from * around and join to the 1st sc. Turn work and work as follows:

First Spoke: **Row 1:** Sl st in next hdc and each of the following 2 dc, sc in next dc, (ch 3, skip next 3 dc, sc in next dc) 7 times, turn. **Row 2:** In 1st lp work a sl st, ch 3 and 3 dc, * 4 dc in next lp, rep from * across, turn. **Row 3:** Skip 1st dc, sl st in each of the next 3 dc, sc in next dc, * ch 3, skip next 3 dc, sc in the next dc, rep from * across to within last 2 dc and the ch-3, turn. **Rows 4, 5, 6:** Rep Rows 2, 3 and 2 in this order. **Row 7:** Skip the 1st dc, sl st in each of the next 3 dc, sc in the next dc, ch 3, skip next 3 dc, sc in next dc, turn. **Row 8:** Work a sl st, ch 3 and 3 dc in lp. Fasten off.

Next Four Spokes: **Row 1:** With wrong side of last row facing and counting from marker following previous spoke, skip the next sc, the hdc and the following dc, then attach thread to next dc, ch 1, sc in next dc, (ch 3, skip next 3 dc, sc in next dc) 7 times, turn. **Next 7 Rows:** Rep Rows 2 through 8 of the 1st spoke and fasten off. Remove all markers.

First Scallop: Make a hairpin lace strip, having 36 lps on each side of the strip. Working along one side of the strip, attach thread to the 1st lp. **Row 1:** Ch 1, sc through the 1st 2 lps (sc through next 2 lps) 17 times, ch 3, turn. **Row 2:** Skip 1st sc, then holding back on hk the last lp of each dc, dc in each of the next 17 sc, thread over and draw carefully through all 18 lps on hk, ch 1 to fasten (cluster made). Fasten off. **Row 3:** With wrong side of cluster facing and working along the opposite side of the strip, attach thread to the 1st lp, ch 1, sc through the same lp, * ch 3, sc through the next lp, rep from * across—35 ch-3 lps, ch 3, turn. **Row 4** (Right Side): * Work 3 dc in next lp, dc in next sc, rep from * across—141 dc, counting the ch 3 as 1 dc, ch 1, turn. **Row 5:** Sc in 1st dc, * ch 3, skip next 3 dc, sc in next dc, rep from * across—35 lps. Fasten off.

Next Three Scallops: Work exactly as for 1st scallop until Row 4 has been completed. **Row 5:** Work as for Row 5 of 1st scallop until 30 lps have been completed, then (ch 1, sl st in corresponding lp of previous scallop, ch 1, skip next 3 dc of scallop in work, sc in next dc) 5 times. Fasten off.

Fifth Scallop: Work as for 1st scallop until Row 4 has been completed, then work Row 5 as before, joining 1st 5 lps to corresponding lps of 1st scallop and last 5 lps to corresponding lps of 4th scallop to form a ring. Fasten off.

Pin ring around spokes, having cluster of each ring meet tip of each spoke and center between each scallop meet center between each spoke. Sew in place.

Next Hairpin Lace Strip: Make a strip of hairpin lace, having 270 lps on each side of strip. Continue now in rnds as follows: **Rnd 6:** With right side facing, attach thread to 1st free lp of any scallop, ch 1, sc in same lp, * (ch 3, sc in next lp) 3 times, (ch 1, sc through next 3 lps of strip, ch 1, sc in next lp of doily) 18 times, (ch 3, sc in next lp of doily) 3 times, ch 3, sc in next free lp of next scallop, rep from * around, ending with ch 3. Join and fasten off. Do not join strip at center. **Rnd 7:** Working along the opposite side of the strip, skip 1st 6 lps of strip, make a lp on hk, * sc through the next 6 lps, (ch 3, sc through the next lp) 30 times, ch 3, sc through the next 6 lps, ch 10, sc through the next 12 lps, ch 10, rep from * around, ending with ch 10, insert hk through last and 1st 6 lps and complete an sc, ch 10, join to 1st sc. Join strip at center. **Rnd 8:** In 1st ch-3 lp work a sl st, ch 3 and 2 dc, * work 3 dc in each ch-3 lp across to within next ch-10 lp, ch 1, (9 sc in next ch-10 lp) twice, ch 1, rep from * around and join to top of ch 3. **Rnd 9:** Ch 1, sc in joining, * (ch 3, skip next 2 dc, sc in next dc) 30 times, ch 3, skip next 2 dc, sc in next ch-1 sp, sl st in each st to within next dc, sc in next dc, rep from * around and join to 1st sc, then sl st to center of 1st lp. Do not fasten off.

Last Hairpin Lace Strip: Make a hairpin lace strip having 340 lps on each side of strip. Continue in rnds as follows: **Rnd 10:** Ch 1, sc through the 1st 6 lps of strip, * ch 1, sc in the same ch-3 lp of doily, ch 3, sc in the next ch-3 lp of doily, (ch 1, sc through next 2 lps of strip, ch 1, sc in next ch-3 lp of doily) 28 times, ch 3, sc in next ch-3 lp of doily, ch 1, sc through the next 6 lps of strip, ch 1, sc in same ch-3 lp of doily. Fasten off, then attach thread again to next ch-3 lp of doily, ch 1, and sc through the next 6 lps of the strip. Rep from * around and fasten off. Do not join strip at center. **Rnd 11:** Work as for the 7th rnd, repeating directions in parentheses 44 times instead of 30 times. Join strip at center. **Rnd 12:** Rep Rnd 8. **Rnd 13:** Ch 1, sc in joining, * (ch 3, skip next 2 sts, sc in next dc) 44 times, ch 3, skip 2 dc, sc in next ch, (ch 3, skip 2 sc, sc in next sc) twice, ch 3, skip 2 sc, draw up a lp in next sc, skip following sc, draw up a lp in next sc, thread over and draw through all 3 lps on hk, (ch 3, skip 2 sc, sc in next sc) twice, ch 3, skip next sc and following ch, sc in next dc. Rep from * around, ending with ch 1 and a hdc in 1st sc to form the last lp. **Rnd 14:**

Ch 1, sc in lp just formed, * ch 4, sc in 3rd ch from hk, ch 1, sc in next lp, rep from * around. Join and fasten off. Starch piece and press into shape.

LACE CIRCLES
As shown on page 109

Design and directions courtesy of D.M.C. Corporation

Tablecloth measures approximately 86 x 100 inches, excluding fringe.

MATERIALS: D.M.C. Crochet Superba, Art. 163, size 10: 95 balls. Steel crochet hook No. 9. Adjustable hairpin loom.

Large Motif: Adjusting the loom to 3 inches, make a strip of hairpin lace with 150 lps on each side. **Rnd 1:** Crochet across the hairpin lace as follows: Insert crochet hk through the 1st 5 lps and work 2 sc in the lp formed, * insert hk through the next 5 lps and work 2 sc in that lp, rep from * around and join with a sl st in the 1st sc to form a ring, then fasten off. Sew the 1st and last sts of the hairpin lace strip firmly together. **Rnd 2 (Right Side):** Working on the opposite free edge of the hairpin lace, insert hk through the 1st 10 lps, draw the last 5 lps through the 1st 5 lps (see Arrow A on drawing, p. 109), * insert the hk through the next 5 lps and draw these 5 lps through the 5 lps already on the hk (Arrow B), rep from * around and join as follows: Place the 5-lp group on hk over the post of the 1st group and with a small piece of thread tie the last group firmly to the post of the 1st group—30 groups on the rnd. **Rnd 3:** Working from the wrong side now, insert hk around the post of any 5-lp group and work 1 sc, ch 7, then * insert hk around the post of the next 5-lp group and work 1 sc, ch 7 and rep from * around. Join in the 1st sc and fasten off.

Flower: Work all rnds from the same side. Ch 2, work 8 sc in the 2nd ch from hk, join in the 1st sc. **Rnd 2:** Ch 1, work 2 sc in the joined sc, ch 4, sl st in the last sc made (picot), * work 2 sc in the next sc, ch 4, sl st in the last sc made, rep from * around (8 picots), join and fasten off. **Rnd 3:** Work 1 sc in the joined sc, * ch 15, sl st in the 2nd ch from hk, sl st in each of the next 12 ch, then leaving the last ch free (stem made) and keeping the next picot in front of work, work 1 sc in the next sc between the picots, rep from * around and join (8 stems). **Rnd 4:** Skip the joined st, * sl st in the 1st ch of the foundation ch on the next stem, then working up the stem, work 1 sc in each of the next 3 sts, hdc in each of the next 2 sts, dc in each of the next 5 sts, hdc in the next st, sc in the next st, 3 sc in the ch at top of stem, then working along the other side, work 1 sc in the 1st sl st, 1 hdc in the next st, dc in each of the 5 sts, hdc in each of 2 sts, sc in each of 3 sts, sl st in the next st (petal made), sl st in the next sc between the next picots, rep from * around, join and fasten off. **Rnd 5:** Sl st in the back lp of the 1st dc on any petal, then working around petal, work ch 1 and 1 sl st in the back lp of each st up to and including the last dc on the other side of the petal, sl st in the back lp of the 1st dc on the next petal, then continue around in the same manner, join and fasten off. Sew flower in place in center of the right side of motif. Block motif to 6½ inches and press. Make 195 more large motifs. Arrange motifs in place as shown in photograph, tacking them together where indicated by the dots on the drawing.

Small Motif: Work and attach small motif in place as follows: Ch 7, join with a sl st to form ring, ch 1, work 1 sc in center of ring, ch 5, sl st in center ch of 1st free ch-7 lp before joining of large motifs (A on drawing), ch 5, sl st in center ch of 1st free ch-7 lp after joining on next large motif (B), ch 5, work 3 sc in center of ring, ch 5, sl st in center ch of next ch-7 lp (C), ch 5, sl st in center ch of 1st free ch-7 lp on next motif (D), ch 5, work 3 sc in center of ring, ch 5, sl st in center ch of next ch-7 lp (E), sl st in center ch of next ch-7 lp on next motif (F), ch 5, work 2 sc in center of ring, join to 1st sc and fasten off. Work and attach all small motifs in the same manner.

Fringe: Cut several strands of thread, each to measure 9 inches. Tie a 9-strand fringe into each free ch-7 lp along the 4 sides of the cloth. Trim ends evenly. Block and press finished piece.

SUNBURST
As shown on page 113

Design and directions courtesy of Scovill Manufacturing Company

Each motif measures 5½ inches square. Afghan measures 45 x 56 inches.

MATERIALS: Knitting Worsted: 8 4-ounce skeins. Hero Aluminum crochet hooks No. E for hairpin lace and No. J for remainder of work. Hero adjustable hairpin loom.

GAUGE: 6 ch-3 and 3 dc patterns = 1 inch

Hairpin Lace Motif: Adjusting the loom to 3½ inches, make 28 for the afghan and 1 for the pillow. Make a strip of hairpin lace with 20 lps on each side. Fasten off, leaving a 12" end. Remove lace from loom, thread the end of the yarn into a tapestry needle and draw tightly through both ends of the spine to form a circle. Fasten off securely.

Edging: **Row 1:** * Sc through 2 lps of the motif, ch 5, sc through 2 lps for corner, (ch 3, sc through 1 lp) twice, ch 3, rep from * around and end with ch 3 and a sl st in the 1st sc. **Row 2:** Sl st in the top of the ch-5, ch 3, work 2 dc in the ch-5 sp, ch 3, work 3 dc in the same sp, * (ch 1, 3 dc in the next sp) 3 times, ch 1, 3 dc, ch 3 and 3 dc in the corner sp, rep from * around and end with a sl st in the top of the starting ch-3. Fasten off.

Joining Motifs: Using an overcast stitch, sew

6 motifs together, 2 motifs wide by 3 motifs long for center of afghan, then make 2 strips each 7 motifs long and 2 strips by 4 motifs long. Join strips of 4 motifs between the two long strips at top and bottom edges, thus forming a rectangle around center of afghan.

Border Around Center: With No. J hk, join yarn in one corner of the center motif piece, ch 3, work 2 dc, ch 3 and 3 dc in any corner, * ch 1, work 3 dc in the next sp, rep from * to next corner, ch 1, 3 dc, ch 3 and 3 dc in that corner, rep from * around and end ch 1 and sl st in top of the starting ch-3. Rep last row 9 times more. Sew the border rectangle of motifs around the last row of crochet, then work another band of crochet in the same manner around the outer edge of the motif rectangle, working for 11 rows. Join at the end of the last row and fasten off.

Fringe: Cut several strands of yarn, each to measure 12 inches. Fold 5 strands in half and draw lp just formed through to wrong side of work, then draw ends through the lp and pull up tight. Make a fringe in each sp around the entire outer edge of the afghan. Trim fringe ends evenly.

Pillow: Starting at one corner sp of the remaining motif, work a crocheted border around it as on the afghan until finished piece measures desired pillow size. Sew the piece over the top of a finished square pillow.

FLORAL PUFFS
As shown on page 113

Design and directions courtesy of Emile Bernat & Sons Company

Each motif measures 5 inches in diameter. Finished afghan measures 44 x 54 inches.

MATERIALS: Bernat Cuddlespun: 6 2-ounce skeins of deep blue (Color A), and 5 each of medium blue (B) and light blue (C). Aluminum crochet hook No. H. Adjustable hairpin loom.

Motifs: Make 40 of each color. Adjusting the loom to 2½ inches, make a strip of hairpin lace with 28 lps on each side. Draw a strand of yarn through the 28 lps at one side of the lace, draw up tightly and fasten off. Form a circle by sewing the ends of the spine together.

Joining Motifs: Following chart below for color arrangement, place 2 motifs side by side. With crochet hook, pick up 1 lp of the right-hand motif on side nearest next motif, pick up 1 lp of 2nd motif and draw through the lp on hk, * pick up next lp of 1st motif and draw through lp on hk, pick up next lp of 2nd motif and draw through lp on hk, rep from * until 7 lps of each motif have been joined, leaving one open lp at the end of the joining. Join 2 more motifs to form a square, always working the joinings toward the center. There will be 4 open lps at the center.

Fill-in Motifs: With Color A, sl st in one open lp, * ch 1, sl st in next lp, rep from * twice more, ch 1, join with a sl st in 1st sl st and fasten off. Continuing to follow chart for color arrangement, make 30 squares of 4 motifs each. Join squares in same manner as before—5 squares (10 motifs) in width and 6 squares (12 motifs) in length, working joinings toward the centers of the squares. After all squares have been joined, there will be 2 open lps and 2 closed lps in each remaining center to be filled in. Work the fill-in motifs for these in the same manner as before.

A = COLOR A   B = COLOR B   C = COLOR C

A	B	C	A	B	B	A	C	B	A
B	C	A	B	C	C	B	A	C	B
C	A	B	C	A	A	C	B	A	C
A	B	C	A	B	B	A	C	B	C
B	C	A	B	C	C	B	A	C	B
C	A	B	C	A	A	C	B	A	C
C	A	B	C	A	A	C	B	A	C
B	C	A	B	C	C	B	A	C	B
A	B	C	A	B	B	A	C	B	A
C	A	B	C	A	A	C	B	A	C
B	C	A	B	C	C	B	A	C	B
A	B	C	A	B	B	A	C	B	A

SCALLOPS OF LACE
As shown on page 115

Design and directions courtesy of Scovill Manufacturing Company

Baby layette is designed for a 6-month size.

MATERIALS: Fingering or baby yarn, 3-ply: 3 ounces for sacque and bonnet, and 6 ounces for blanket. Hero steel crochet hook No. 3. Hero adjustable hairpin loom.

GAUGE: 11 dc = 2 inches and 3 dc rows = 1 inch

SACQUE

Yoke: Starting at neck edge, ch 59. **Row 1:** Dc in 4th ch from hk (the turning ch counts as 1 dc), dc in each of the next 9 ch, 5 dc in the next ch, dc in each of the next 7 ch, 5 dc in the next ch, dc in each of the next 18 ch, 5 dc in the next ch, dc in each of the next 7 ch, 5 dc in the next ch, dc in each of the next 10 ch—56 dc. Ch 3, turn. **Row 2:** Work a dc in each dc and 5 dc in the center dc of each 5-dc group on previous row, ch 3, turn. Rep Row 2 until there are 216 dc, and 10 dc rows have been worked. Ch 3, turn. **Next Row:** Dc in each dc to the 3rd dc of the next 5-dc group, ch 7 for underarm, skip next 47 dc, dc in each of the next 60 dc, ch 7 for underarm, skip next 47 dc, dc in each of the next 31 dc. Ch 1, do not turn. Work in sc now up the front to the neck, ch 3, skip 1 st on the foundation ch, * dc in the next st, ch 1, skip the next st, rep from * across the neck for beading, then work in sc down the opposite front and fasten off.

Hairpin Lace Body: Adjust the loom to 2 inches, then make a strip of lace having 195 lps on each side. Remove lace from loom, ch 8, * (sc through 3 lps, ch 5) 5 times, sc through 15 lps, ch 5, rep from * to end of strip and end with a cluster of 3 loops, then

Hairpin Lace Directions   **159**

ch 8, sc in the spine of the lace, ch 8, ** sc through 15 lps, (ch 5, sc through 3 lps) 5 times, ch 5, rep from ** and end with sc through 15 lps, ch 8, sl st in the end of spine and fasten off. Make 2 more strips in the same manner.

Joining Strips: Join yarn to spine of the 1st strip at the 15-lp cluster, ch 3, sc between the 1st and 2nd cluster of 3 lps on the 2nd strip, ch 3, sc under the ch-8 of the 1st strip next to the 15-lp cluster, * sc under the next ch-5 of the 2nd strip, ch 3, sc under the next ch-5 of the 1st strip, then rep from * and end ch 3 and sc between the last 2 clusters of the 2nd strip. Join the 3rd strip to the 2nd strip in the same manner. Whip stitch one edge of the lace to the lower edge of the yoke. *Sleeves:* Make 2 strips of lace having 90 lps on each side. Work the edge and joining in the same manner as for the body of the sacque, then sew the sleeves in place. *Tie:* Make a twisted cord 20 inches long and draw it through the beading row at the neck edge. Trim the ends of the cord with tiny pompons or tassels.

BONNET

Front: Make 2 strips of lace having 105 lps on each side. Work edges of strips in same manner as for body of sacque, having ch-3 instead of ch-5 between clusters, then join strips in same manner as for sacque.

Back: Ch 4, join with a sl st to form a ring. **Rnd 1:** Ch 3 to count as 1 dc, work 11 dc in the center of the ring, join with a sl st to top of the ch-3, ch 3, turn. **Rnd 2:** Dc in the joining, work 2 dc in each dc around, join to top of the ch-3, ch 3, turn. **Rnd 3:** Dc in joining, * 1 dc in the next dc, 2 dc in the next dc, rep from * around, join to top of the ch-3, ch 3, turn. **Rnd 4:** Work even in dc, join and ch 3 to turn. **Rnd 5:** Dc in joining, * 1 dc in each of the next 2 dc, 2 dc in the next dc, rep from * around, join, ch 3, turn. Continue to inc now as on Rnd 5, having 1 st more between the increases on each row until 8 rows have been worked. **Next Row:** Dc in each st to the last 12 sts and fasten off. These 12 sts are for the back of the neck.

Finishing: Whip st one edge of the lace across the cap from neck edge to neck edge. Work 1 row of sc along the sides and back of neck, ch 5, turn. **Next Row:** * Skip 1 st, dc in the next st, ch 1, rep from * across and end with a dc in the last st for the beading row. Make a twisted cord 20 inches long and draw it through the beading row. Trim the ends with pompons or tassels.

BLANKET

Adjust loom to 3 inches and make a strip of lace having 330 lps on each side. Remove lace from loom, then ch 11, * (sc through 3 lps, ch 3) 5 times along one side of strip, sc through 15 lps, ch 3, rep from * to end, ch 11, sc in center of spine, ch 11, rep from * down opposite side of strip and end ch 11 and join with a sl st in the spine of the lace. Fasten off. Make 7 more strips and join these strips in the same manner as for the sacque, then work 1 row of sc around the outer edge, adjusting the number of sc under the ch-11's to keep the work flat.

DELICATE VINES
As shown on page 116

Design and directions courtesy of Scovill Manufacturing Company

Scarf measures 17 x 70 inches.

MATERIALS: Fingering or baby yarn: 7 ounces. Hero aluminum crochet hook No. C. Hero adjustable hairpin loom.

Strips (Make 6): Adjusting loom to 2½ inches, make a strip of hairpin lace with 540 lps on each side. Do not fasten off yarn but remove strip from loom and * ch 9, then working along one long side, sc through 2 lps, (ch 3, sc through 2 lps) 4 times, ** ch 3, sc through 10 lps, (ch 3, sc through 2 lps) 5 times, rep from ** along edge and end ch 3, sc through 10 lps, ch 9, sl st in center of spine of lace, rep from * along opposite side of strip and end ch 9 and a sl st in center of spine. Fasten off.

Joining Strips: Sc under a ch-9 at the end of the 1st strip next to a 10-cluster group, ch 3, sc in the sp between the 2nd and 3rd 2-lp cluster on the 2nd strip, * ch 3, sc in next sp on 1st strip, ch 3, sc in next sp on 2nd strip, rep from * and end ch 3, sc under the ch-9 on the 2nd strip after the last 10-lp cluster. Fasten off. Join all strips in the same manner.

Fringe: Cut several strands of yarn, each to measure 24 inches. Fold 6 strands in half and draw lp through the ch-9 lp at the start of one short end of the scarf, draw the ends through the lp just formed and pull up tight. Make a fringe in each ch-9 sp and in the center of each joining across each short end of the scarf. Trim fringe ends evenly.

TOSCA
As shown on page 117

Design and directions courtesy of William Unger Co., Inc.

Stole measures 19 x 100 inches; may be made shorter by working fewer strips.

MATERIALS: Unger's Lovely: 8 40-gram balls. Aluminum crochet hook No. F for hairpin lace and edging and No. G for remainder of work. Adjustable hairpin loom.

First Strip (Make 10): Adjusting loom to 2 inches, make a strip of hairpin lace with 81 lps on each side. Fasten off and remove strip from loom.

Crochet Edging: **Row 1:** Attach yarn in 1st lp along one side edge and twisting the lps as you work, work 1 sc into each lp across the strip, ch 3, turn. **Row 2:** Counting the turning ch as the 1st st, dc in the next st, * ch 3, skip 2 sts, work a sl st in the next st, ch 4 and sl st in the same st (picot), ch 3, skip 2 sts, dc in next st, rep from * across and end with 1 dc in the last st—13 picot sts. Ch 2, turn. **Row 3:** Counting the turning ch as the 1st hdc, hdc in the next st, * ch 1, dc under the next ch-3 of the previous row, ch 2, dc under the next ch-3 of the previous row, ch 1, hdc in next dc, rep from * across and end hdc in last st, ch 2, turn. **Row 4:**

Joining Row: Counting the turning ch as the 1st hdc, hdc in the next st, * ch 4 loosely, sc under the next ch-2, ch 4 loosely, sc in the next hdc of previous row, rep from * and end hdc in the last st. Fasten off. Rep Rows 1 through 4 along the opposite edge of the strip.

Second Strip (Make 10): Work as for the 1st strip until Row 3 of the 2nd edge is completed. Join the 2nd strip to the 1st strip as follows: Sc and ch 2 in the 1st st of the 1st strip and ch 2 in the 2nd st of the 2nd strip, sc and ch 2 under the next ch-4 of the 1st strip, * sc and ch 2 under the next ch-2 of the 2nd strip, sc and ch 2 under the next ch-4 of the 1st strip, sc and ch 2 in the next hdc of the 2nd strip, sc and ch 2 under the next ch-4 of the 1st strip. Rep from * across and end sc in the last st of the 1st strip, ch 2, sc in the last st of the 2nd strip. Fasten off. Join 20 strips in this manner.

Finishing: Attach yarn at one corner. Work 1 row of hdc along one long edge, ch 3, turn, then work one row as Row 2 of the 1st strip. Fasten off. Rep these 2 rows along the opposite long edge.

Fringe: Cut several strands of yarn, each to measure 24 inches. Fold 8 strands in half and draw the lp through, then draw all loose ends through the lp just formed and pull up tight. Work a fringe in each lp along each short edge of stole. Trim fringe ends evenly.

LILIOM
As shown on page 118

Design and directions courtesy of William Unger & Co., Inc.

Shawl measures 70 inches across the top and 40 inches through center.

MATERIALS: Unger's Liliom: 10 40-gram balls. Aluminum crochet hook No. F. Adjustable hairpin loom.

Motifs (Make 18): Adjusting loom to 1½ inches, make a strip of hairpin lace with 48 lps on each side. Fasten off. Draw a strand of yarn through all 48 lps along one side of the strip, being careful that the lps twist in the same direction, then draw the strand up tightly and knot the ends, forming a circle with a small hole at the center. Tack these ends together along the spine.

Crochet Joining: Attach yarn to one lp along the outer edge of the circle and ch 1 (counts as 1 st). Keeping the lps twisted in the same direction, work 1 sc in each of the next 11 lps, * ch 4, sc in the 1st ch of the group of 4 for a picot, 1 sc in each of the next 12 lps, rep from * around, and end with a picot. Join with a sl st to the 1st st and fasten off. There are 4 picots evenly spaced around the motif. Work the 2nd motif in the same manner as the 1st until the crochet row, then work as follows: Attach yarn in a lp along the outer edge, ch 1 (counts as 1 st), 1 sc in each of the next 11 lps, work a picot, 1 sc in each of the next 12 lps, ch 2, hold back to back to 1st motif, sl st in a picot of that motif, ch 1, sl st in the 1st ch of 2 chs on the 2nd motif (picot joining), * 1 sc in each of the next 12 lps, work a picot, rep from * around and join with a sl st. Fasten off. There are now 3 free picots and one joined picot. Make and join all 18 motifs into a strip in this manner.

Body of Shawl: **Row 1:** Starting at center top, ch 10, sc in 4th ch from hk (picot formed), dc in 7th ch (1st picot V st), skip 2 ch, ch 2, dc, ch 3, sc into 1st ch of the ch-3 (picot) and dc in the last st, ch 6, turn. **Row 2:** Sc in 4th ch from hk, dc in 1st st, ch 1, dc, ch 3, sc in 1st ch of ch-3 (picot) and dc in the next sp under the ch-2, ch 2, dc, ch 3, sc in 1st ch of ch-3, and dc under the same ch-2 (ch 2 is center of shawl), ch 1, dc, ch 3, sc in 1st ch and dc in the end st (picot V st). There are now 4 picot V sts on the row. Ch 6, turn. **Row 3:** Sc in 4th ch from hk, dc back in 1st st, ch 1, picot V st under the next ch-1, ch 1, picot V st under the ch-2, ch 2, picot V st back under the same ch-2, ch 1, picot V st under the next ch-1, ch 1, picot V st in the end st— 6 picot V sts. Ch 6, turn. **Row 4:** Sc in 4th ch from hk, dc back in 1st st, (ch 1, picot V st under the next ch-1) twice, ch 1, picot V st under the ch-2 at center, ch 2, picot V st under the same ch-2 at center, (ch 1, picot V st under the next ch-1) twice, ch 1, picot V st in the end st—8 picot V sts. Ch 6, turn. Continue in this manner working 1 picot V st more on each side of the center ch-2 until there are 44 picot V sts on each side—88 picot V sts on the row.

Joining Motif Border to Shawl: **Next Row:**

Inc on this picot V row as on previous rows. Work 2 picot V sts, ch 1, dc under the next ch-1, ch 1, sl st in a top outside picot of the 1st motif, ch 1, and sc back to the 1st ch-1, dc back under the same ch-1 (picot V st joining), * ch 1, (picot V st, ch 1) 4 times, dc under the next ch-1, ch 1, sl st in next top outside picot on the next motif, ch 1, sc back in the 1st ch-1 (picot V st joining). Rep from * around the entire outer edge and end with 2 picot V sts. Fasten off.

Inserts: Ch 4, join with a sl st to form a ring. **Rnd 1:** Ch 1, work 9 sc in center of ring and join with a sl st. **Rnd 2:** *Joining Rnd:* Sc in the 1st st, place the piece in center between 2 attached motifs, ch 3, count 6 lps from a joining picot on the shawl to a motif, sl st in the 6th lp on the 1st motif, ch 3, sc back into the next sc on the insert, work 1 sc in each of the next 2 sc, ch 3, sl st in the 6th lp from the picot on the shawl joining to the 2nd motif, ch 3, sc into the next st on the insert, work 1 sc in each of the next 2 sc, ch 4, sl st in the center ch sp of 4 picot V sts on the shawl (ch sp is between the 2nd and 3rd picot V sts), ch 4, sc in next sc on the insert, sc in the next st, join with a sl st and fasten off. Work an insert between 2 motifs along each side of the shawl except at point of V and the sides.

Side Joining: Attach yarn in 1st picot V st, ch 6, then counting 6 lps on the motif from the shawl picot joining, sl st in the sp between the lps, ch 6, sl st back in the 1st picot V st, ch 13, sl st in the picot at the side edge of the motif, ch 13, sl st back in the 1st picot V st and fasten off. Be sure that all pieces lay flat. *V Insert:* Work as for other inserts, working ch 1 instead of ch 3 and ch 2 instead of ch 4.

Edging: Attach yarn in picot at one side edge, ch 1, work 1 sc in each of the next 6 sts along the outer edge of the 1st motif, ch 4, sc in the next st and in each of the next 5 sts, ch 4, work 1 sc in each of the next 6 sts on the motif, ch 4, work 1 sc in each of the next 6 sts on the motif, dc in center of the picot joining, ch 2, dc back into same place, * work 1 sc in each of the next 6 sts of the next motif, ch 4, (work 1 sc in each of the next 6 sts, ch 4) twice, 1 sc in each of the next 6 sts, dc in center of the picot joining, ch 2, dc in same place, rep from * around and end with 1 sc in the last picot at the other side edge. Fasten off.

Fringe: Cut several strands of yarn, each to measure 24 inches. Fold 6 strands in half and draw through a ch-4 lp on the outer edge of shawl. Draw loose ends through the lp formed and pull up tight. Work a fringe in each ch-4 lp and in each dc, ch 2 and dc V st along the edges of the shawl as shown. Trim ends evenly.

PINWHEELS
As shown on page 119

Design and directions courtesy of Scovill Manufacturing Company

Each motif measures 5¾ inches square. Shawl

measures 47 inches square, excluding fringe.

MATERIALS: Mohair: 16 1-ounce balls. Hero aluminum crochet hook No. G. Hero adjustable hairpin loom.

Motifs (Make 64): Adjusting loom to 2½ inches and with double strands of yarn, make a strip of hairpin lace with 20 lps on each side. Cut yarn, leaving a 12-inch end and remove lace from loom. Thread end in tapestry needle, draw through the lps at the short edge to form a circle and fasten securely. Sew the ends of the spine together.

Edging: Attach yarn to any lp of the motif. **Rnd 1:** * Ch 3, work 1 sc in the next lp, rep from * around and join with a sl st in 1st sc—20 sc. **Rnd 2:** Work ch 4, 1 tr c, ch 3 and 2 tr c in joining for corner, * in next sc work tr c, dc and hdc, in next sc work hdc and 2 sc, ch 1, in next sc work 2 sc and hdc, in next sc work hdc, dc and tr c, in next sc work 2 tr c, ch 3 and 2 tr c for corner, rep from * around and end at 4th sc of the last side. Join with a sl st in the top of the starting ch-4 and fasten off.

Joining Motifs: Holding pieces with right sides together, and working through only 1 lp of each st, sew edges together with an overcast st, starting at the center of one corner lp and ending at the center of the next corner lp. Join the motifs together now to form a long strip of 8 motifs. Make another long strip in the same manner.

Fringe: Cut several strands of yarn, each to measure 16 inches. Fold 6 strands in half.

Draw lp through the ch 3 at one corner, draw ends through the lp and pull up tight. Make a fringe in the center st of each group of sts around the entire outer edge of the shawl. On the right side knot 3 strands of the 1st fringe with 3 strands of the adjacent fringe approximately ¾ inch below the 1st knots. Make another row of knots using 3 strands from the 2nd fringe with 3 strands from the adjacent fringe and knotting again approximately ¾ inch below the 2nd row of knots. Trim fringe ends evenly.

BOUQUET

As shown on page 121

Design and directions courtesy of Scovill Manufacturing Company

Each strip measures 3½ inches in width before joining. Skirt has been designed for small size (6–8). Changes for medium (10–12) and large (14–16) are in parentheses.

MATERIALS: Knitting worsted: 6 4-ounce skeins. Hero aluminum crochet hook No. E. Hero adjustable hairpin loom.

GAUGE: 1 pattern of 42 lps = 6 inches

Strips (Make 9): Adjusting loom to 3 inches, make a strip of hairpin lace with 294 (336, 378) lps on each side. Fasten off.

Edging: Being careful not to twist lps, * work 1 sc through 21 lps on one side of strip, ch 5, (sc through next 3 lps, ch 5) 7 times, rep from * across and end ch 5, join with a sl st in 1st sc to form a circle and fasten off. **Row 2:** Rep Row 1 along opposite edge of strip. Sew the ends of the spine together to form motif.

Note: When working the 2nd row of the last strip, work ch 3 instead of ch 5 between lps to tighten at waist edge.

Joining Motifs: Sc under the ch-5 before a cluster of 21 lps, ch 2, sc under the ch-5 before the 4th cluster of 3 lps on the 2nd motif, * ch 2, sc under the next ch-5 of the 1st motif, ch 2, sc under the next ch-5 of the 2nd motif, rep from * around and end ch 2, sl st in the 1st sc and fasten off. Join each motif in the same manner.

Finishing: Waistband: Work 3 rnds of sc around one edge for waist, holding in the 1st row slightly and joining at the end of each rnd. **Next Rnd:** *Beading Rnd:* Ch 5, * skip 2 sc, dc in the next sc, ch 2, rep from * around and join in the 3rd st of the starting ch-5. Work 3 more rnds of sc and fasten off. To finish the lower edge, work 1 rnd of sc, working 4 sc under each ch-5 and 1 sc in each sc. *Cord:* With double strands of yarn, crochet a chain to measure 72 inches or desired length. Weave chain through the beading row.

Tassels: (Make 2): Wind yarn 80 times around an 8-inch piece of cardboard and tie the strands together at one end. Remove from cardboard. With a separate strand of yarn, wind yarn 10 times 1 inch below tie and tie again. Clip the other end and trim evenly. Sew one tassel to each end of the cord.

 # NINE

Knitting Directions

HOW TO KNIT

HOW TO CAST ON

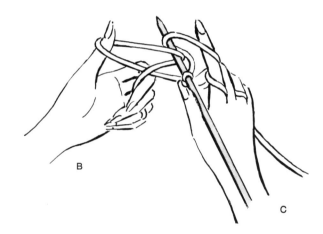

Make a loop on needle, allowing a 2-yard end of yarn for every 100 stitches that need to be cast on, more if your yarn is a heavier than average weight, and less if it is lighter. This is your first stitch (A).

Hold needle in your right hand with short end of yarn toward you, then * (1) with short end make a loop on left thumb and insert needle from front to back through this loop (B). (2) Place yarn attached to ball under and around needle (C).

D

(3) Draw yarn through loop and pull short end down to tighten it (D). (4) Repeat from * for desired number of stitches.

THE KNIT STITCH

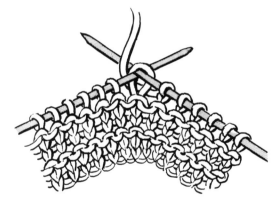

Holding needle with cast-on stitches in your left hand with yarn to back of work, * insert right needle from left to right through front of first stitch, wrap yarn completely around right needle forming a loop, slip needle and loop through stitch to front, and slip stitch just worked off left needle. This is your first knit stitch. Repeat from * in same manner across all stitches on left needle.

THE PURL STITCH

* Holding yarn in front of work, insert right needle from right to left through front of first stitch on left needle, wrap yarn completely around right needle, forming a loop, slip needle and loop through stitch to back, and slip stitch just worked off left needle. Repeat from * until all stitches are worked.

HOW TO INCREASE

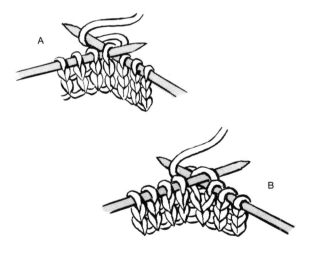

A

B

Insert right needle from right to left through back of next stitch on left needle, wrap yarn completely around needle, forming a loop (A), and slip needle and loop through to front, forming a new stitch on right needle, then knit the same stitch on left needle in usual manner (B), and slip the stitch from left needle.

HOW TO DECREASE

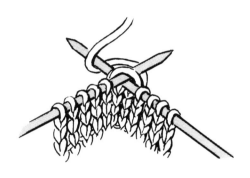

Insert right needle through 2 stitches on left needle and work these stitches together as one stitch.

THE YARN OVER

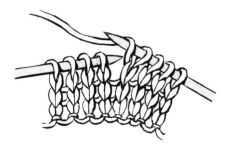

When knitting, wrap yarn under and around right needle as shown, forming a loop. When purling, wrap yarn over and around right needle, then work next stitch in either case as indicated in pattern being worked, thus adding a simulated stitch to form an eyelet hole.

HOW TO PICK UP STITCHES

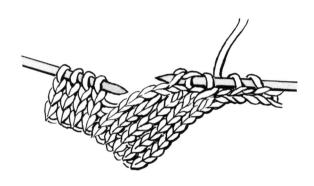

Picking up stitches, as is necessary around a neck or an armhole, is always done on the right side of work, usually starting at a seam edge, such as the top of one shoulder for neck stitches, or at the underarm for an armhole shaping. Stitches are picked up by inserting your right needle through center of desired stitch and knitting that stitch in usual manner onto right needle, fitting the number of stitches evenly into the complete space available for the picking up of your stitches.

HOW TO BIND OFF

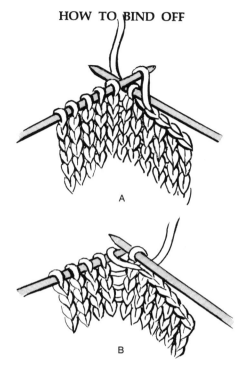

A

B

Knit first 2 stitches, then * insert point of left needle into the 1st stitch on right needle (A) and lift this stitch over the 2nd stitch and drop off needle (B). Knit another stitch and repeat from * across for necessary number of stitches to be bound off. When all stitches are to be bound off at the end of a piece of work, and when one stitch remains, break off yarn and fasten off by drawing remaining yarn through that last stitch.

Abbreviations

beg	beginning
dec	decrease
inc	increase

k	knit
psso	pass slip stitch over
p	purl
rep	repeat
sl st	slip stitch
tog	together
yo	yarn over
*	indicates directions following are to be repeated as necessary

VICTORIANA

As shown on page 96

Design and directions courtesy of Coats & Clark, Inc.

Insertion measures 2¾ inches wide. Edging measures 3¾ inches wide. Dinner cloth measures 69 x 90 inches, including fringe.

Note: *This dinner cloth was designed almost 100 years ago and has retained its simple charm through the years.*

MATERIALS: Clark's Big Ball Mercerized Crochet Art. B.34, size 30: 11 balls. Straight knitting needles No. 1. Linen or other material: 2¼ yards, 72 inches wide.

Insertions: Make 2 strips each to measure 61½ inches long, 2 strips each 59 inches long, and 4 strips each 9 inches long. Starting at narrow edge, cast on 25 sts and k 1 row. Now work in pattern as follows: **Row 1 (Right Side):** K 2, k 2 tog, yo, k 7, yo, sl 1, k 2 tog, psso, yo, k 5, k 2 tog, yo, k 4. Mark the 1st pattern row for right side. **Row 2 and All Even Rows Unless Otherwise Specified:** K 2, k 2 tog, yo, k 15, k 2 tog, yo, k 4. **Row 3:** K 2, k 2 tog, yo, k 5, k 2 tog, yo, k 3, yo, sl 1, k 1, psso, k 3, k 2 tog, yo, k 4. **Row 5:** K 2, k 2 tog, yo, k 4, k 2 tog, yo, k 5, yo, sl 1, k 1, psso, k 2, k 2 tog, yo, k 4. **Row 7:** K 2, k 2 tog, yo, k 3, k 2 tog, yo, k 7, yo, sl 1, k 1, psso, k 1, k 2 tog, yo, k 4. **Row 9:** (K 2, k 2 tog, yo) 3 times, sl 1, k 1, psso, k 3, yo, sl 1, k 1, psso, k 2 tog, yo, k 4—24 sts. **Row 10:** K 2, k 2 tog, yo, k 8, k and p in next yo, k 5, k 2 tog, yo, k 4—25 sts. **Row 11:** K 2, k 2 tog, yo, k 4, yo, sl 1, k 1, psso, k 5, k 2 tog, yo, k 2, k 2 tog, yo, k 4. **Row 13:** K 2, k 2 tog, yo, k 5, yo, sl 1, k 1, psso, k 3, k 2 tog, yo, k 3, k 2 tog, yo, k 4. **Row 15:** K 2, k 2 tog, yo, k 6, yo, sl 1, k 1, psso, k 1, (k 2 tog, yo, k 4) twice. **Row 16:** Rep Row 2. Rep Rows 1 through 16 for pattern. Work in pattern for indicated length and end with Row 2 of pattern. Bind off. Block strips to measurements.

Cut linen in the following manner: Trim selvedge from each long edge. From the length of linen, cut 2 pieces, each 10 x 60 inches, and one piece 39 x 60 inches. From remaining linen cut 2 pieces, each to measure 10 x 39 inches, and 4 10-inch squares. Sew a ¼-inch hem around each piece of linen, mitering the corners. Press the hem, then following diagram below, sew insertions in place.

Edging: Starting at narrow edge, cast on 29 sts and k 1 row, then work in pattern as follows: **Row 1** (Right Side): K 2, k 2 tog, yo, k 7, yo, sl 1, k 2 tog, psso, yo, k 2, k 2 tog, yo, sl 1, k 1, psso, k 3, yo, sl 1, k 2 tog,

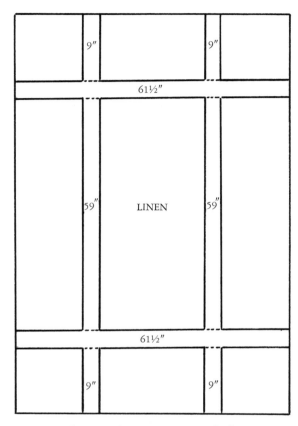

psso, yo, k 2 tog, k 1—27 sts. Mark the 1st pattern row for right side. **Row 2:** Yo, k 2 tog, k 7, k and p in the next yo, k to within the last 6 sts, k 2 tog, yo, k 4—28 sts. **Row 3:** K 2, k 2 tog, yo, k 5, k 2 tog, yo, k 3, yo, sl 1, k 1, psso, k 5, k 2 tog, yo, k 3, yo, k 2— 29 sts. **Row 4 and All Even Rows Unless Otherwise Specified:** Yo, k 2 tog, k across to within the last 6 sts, k 2 tog, yo, k 4. **Row 5:** K 2, k 2 tog, yo, k 4, k 2 tog, yo, k 5, yo, sl 1, k 1, psso, k 3, k 2 tog, yo, k 5, yo, k 2—30 sts. **Row 7:** K 2, k 2 tog, yo, k 3, k 2 tog, yo, k 7, yo, sl 1, k 1, psso, k 1, k 2 tog, yo, k 7, yo, k 2—31 sts. **Row 9:** (K 2, k 2 tog, yo) 3 times, sl 1, k 1, psso, k 3, yo, sl 1, k 2 tog, psso, yo, k 2, k 2 tog, yo, sl 1, k 1, psso, k 3, yo, k 2—30 sts. **Row 10:** Yo, k 2 tog, k 5, k and p in the next yo, k 10, k and p in the next yo, k 5, k 2 tog, yo, k 4—32 sts. **Row 11:** K 2, k 2 tog, yo, k 4, yo, sl 1, k 1, psso, k 5, k 2 tog, yo, k 3, yo, sl 1, k 1, psso, k 5, k 2 tog, yo, k 2 tog, k 1—31 sts. **Row 13:** K 2, k 2 tog, yo, (k 5, yo, sl 1, k 1, psso, k 3, k 2 tog, yo) twice, k 2 tog, k 1—30 sts. **Row 15:** K 2, k 2 tog, yo, k 6, yo, sl 1, k 1, psso, k 1, k 2 tog, yo, k 7, yo, sl 1, k 1, psso, k 1, k 2 tog, yo, k 2 tog, k 1—29 sts. **Row 16:** Rep Row 4. Rep Rows 1 through 16 for pattern. Continue now to work in pattern until edging reaches around entire outer edge of the cloth, allowing 5 inches more for each of the 4 corners and ending with Row 2 of pattern. Bind off.

Block to measurements. Sew narrow edges together. Pin the knitted edging around the outer edge of the cloth, easing in 5 extra inches at each corner. Sew in place.

MILLPOND

As shown on page 106

Design and directions courtesy of Coats & Clark, Inc.

Doily measures 19 inches square from scallop to scallop.

MATERIALS: Clark's Big Ball Mercerized Crochet, Art. B.34, size 20: 2 balls; or Art. B.345, size 20: 1 ball. 5 10-inch double-pointed needles No. 0.

Center: Starting at center, cast on 8 sts.

Divide sts on 4 needles, having 2 sts on each needle, and join, being careful not to twist sts. **Rnd 1:** K. **Rnd 2:** (K in the front and back of the next st) 8 times—16 sts. **Rnd 3:** K. **Rnd 4:** (Yo, k 3, yo, k 1) 4 times—24 sts, counting each yo as 1 st. **Rnd 5:** (Yo, k 5, yo, k 1) 4 times—32 sts.

Note: From this point on, work the directions as given once across each of the 4 needles. The number of sts given at the end of a rnd is for each of the 4 needles. **Rnd 6:** K. **Rnd 7 (Inc Rnd):** Yo, k to within last st on the same needle, yo, k 1—10 sts. **Rnd 8 (Inc Rnd):** Rep Rnd 7. There are now 2 sts more on each needle than on the previous inc rnd. Rep Rnds 6, 7, and 8 until there are 76 sts on each needle. **Next Rnd:** K.

Border: **Rnd 1:** Yo, k 2, (k 2 tog, yo, sl 1, k 1, psso, k 2 tog, yo, sl 1, k 1, psso, k 1) 8 times, k 1, yo, k 1—62 sts. **Rnd 2:** K 4 (k and p in next yo, k 2, k and p in next yo, k 3) 8 times, then k the last 2 sts—78 sts. **Rnd 3:** Yo, k 2 tog, yo, k 1, (yo, sl 1, k 1, psso, k 2 tog, yo, sl 1, k 1, psso, k 2 tog, yo, k 1) 8 times, then yo, sl 1, k 1, psso, yo, k 1—72 sts. **Rnd 4:** K 7 (k and p in next yo, k 7) 8 times, k the last st—80 sts. **Rnd 5:** Yo, k 1, yo, (sl 1, k 1, psso, k 1, k 2 tog, yo, sl 1, k 1, psso, k 2 tog, yo) 8 times, then sl 1, k 1, psso, k 1, k 2 tog, (yo, k 1) twice—66 sts. **Rnd 6:** K 6 (k and p in next yo, k 2, k and p in next yo, k 3) 8 times, then k the last 4 sts—82 sts. **Rnd 7:** Yo, k 2, (k 2 tog, yo, k 1, yo, sl 1, k 1, psso, k 2 tog, yo, sl 1, k 1, psso) 8 times, then k 2 tog, yo, k 1, yo, sl 1, k 1, psso, k 2, yo, k 1—76 sts. **Rnd 8:** K 5, (k and p in next st, k 3, k and p in next yo, k 3) 8 times, k and p in next st, k 6—92 sts. **Rnd 9:** Yo, k 1, yo, (k 3, k 2 tog, yo, sl 1, k 1, psso, k 3, yo) 9 times, k 1, yo, k 1—96 sts. **Rnd 10 and All Even Rnds Unless Otherwise Specified:** K. **Rnd 11:** Yo, k 2 tog, (yo, k 1, yo, sl 1, k 1, psso, k 5, k 2 tog) 9 times, then yo, k 1, yo, sl 1, k 1, psso, yo, k 1—98 sts. **Rnd 13:** Yo, k 2 tog, (yo, k 3, yo, sl 1, k 1, psso, k 3, k 2 tog) 9 times, then yo, k 3, yo, sl 1, k 1, psso, yo, k 1—100 sts. **Rnd 15:** Yo, k 2 tog, (yo, k 1, yo, sl 1, k 2 tog, psso, yo, k 1, yo, sl 1, k 1, psso, k 1, k 2 tog) 9 times, then yo, k 1, yo, sl 1, k 2 tog, psso, yo, k 1, yo, sl 1, k 1, psso, yo, k 1—102 sts. **Rnd 17:** Yo, k 2 tog, yo, sl 1, k 2 tog, psso, * yo, k 1, (yo, sl 1, k 2 tog, psso) 3 times, rep from * 8 times more, then yo, k 1, yo, sl 1, k 2 tog, psso, yo, sl 1, k 1, psso, yo, k 1—84 sts. **Rnd 19:** Yo, k 4, * yo, (sl 1, k 2 tog, psso, yo, k 1, yo) twice, sl 1, k 2 tog, psso, yo, k 5, rep from * 4 times more and end last repeat with k 4 instead of k 5, yo, k 1—86 sts. **Rnd 21:** Yo, k 7, (yo, sl 1, k 2 tog, psso, yo, k 1, yo, sl 1, k 2 tog, psso, yo, k 9) 4 times, yo, sl 1, k 2 tog, psso, yo, k 1, yo, sl 1, k 2 tog, psso, yo, k 7, yo, k 1—88 sts. **Rnd 23:** Yo, k 4, yo, (sl 1, k 1, psso, k 4, yo, sl 1, k 2 tog, psso, yo, k 4, k 2 tog, yo, k 1, yo) 4 times, sl 1, k 1, psso, k 4, yo, sl 1, k 2 tog, psso, yo, k 4, k 2 tog, yo, k 4, yo, k 1—90 sts. **Rnd 25:** Yo, k 4, yo, (sl 1, k 1, psso, yo, sl 1, k 1, psso, k 9, k 2 tog, yo, k 2 tog, yo, k 1, yo, sl 1, k 1, psso,

k 9, k 2 tog, yo, k 1, yo) twice, then sl 1, k 1, psso, yo, sl 1, k 1, psso, k 9, k 2 tog, yo, k 2 tog, yo, k 4, yo, k 1—92 sts. **Rnd 27:** Yo, k 4, * (yo, sl 1, k 1, psso) 3 times, k 7, (k 2 tog, yo) 3 times, k 1, yo, sl 1, k 1, psso, k 7, k 2 tog, yo, k 1, rep from * once more then (yo, sl 1, k 1, psso) 3 times, k 7 (k 2 tog, yo) 3 times, k 4, yo, k 1—94 sts. **Rnd 29:** Yo, k 4, * (yo, sl 1, k 1, psso) 4 times, k 5, (k 2 tog, yo) 4 times, k 1, yo, sl 1, k 1, psso, k 5, k 2 tog, yo, k 1, rep from * once more, then (yo, sl 1, k 1, psso) 4 times, k 5, (k 2 tog, yo) 4 times, k 4, yo, k 1—96 sts. **Rnd 31:** Yo, k 4, * (yo, sl 1, k 1, psso) 5 times, k 3, (k 2 tog, yo) 5 times, k 1, yo, sl 1, k 1, psso, k 3, k 2 tog, yo, k 1, rep from * once more, then (yo, sl 1, k 1, psso) 5 times, k 3, (k 2 tog, yo) 5 times, k 4, yo, k 1—98 sts. **Rnd 33:** Yo, k 4, * (yo, sl 1, k 1, psso) 6 times, k 1, (k 2 tog, yo) 6 times, k 1, yo, sl 1, k 1, psso, k 1, k 2 tog, yo, k 1, rep from * once more, then (yo, sl 1, k 1, psso) 6 times, k 1, (k 2 tog, yo) 6 times, k 4, yo, k 1—100 sts. **Rnd 35:** Yo, k 4, * (yo, sl 1, k 1, psso) 6 times, yo, sl 1, k 2 tog, psso, yo, (k 2 tog, yo) 6 times, k 1, yo, sl 1, k 2 tog, psso, yo, k 1 rep from * once more, then (yo, sl 1, k 1, psso) 6 times, yo, sl 1, k 2 tog, psso, yo, (k 2 tog, yo) 6 times, k 4, yo, k 1—102 sts. **Rnd 37:** Yo, k 4, * (yo, sl 1, k 1, psso) 7 times, k 1 (k 2 tog, yo) 7 times, k 3 and rep from * once more, then (yo, sl 1, k 1, psso) 7 times, k 1, (k 2 tog, yo) 7 times, k 4, yo, k 1—104 sts. **Rnd 39:** Yo, k 6, * (yo, sl 1, k 1, psso) 6 times, yo, sl 1, k 2 tog, psso, yo, (k 2 tog, yo) 6 times, k 5, rep from * once more, (yo, sl 1, k 1, psso) 6 times, yo, sl 1, k 2 tog, psso, yo, (k 2 tog, yo) 6 times, k 6, yo, k 1—106 sts. **Rnd 41:** Yo, k 8, * (yo, sl 1, k 1, psso) 6 times, k 1, (k 2 tog, yo) 6 times, k 7 and rep from * once more, then (yo, sl 1, k 1, psso) 6 times, k 1 (k 2 tog, yo) 6 times, k 8, yo, k 1—108 sts. **Rnd 43:** Yo, k 10, * (yo, sl 1, k 1, psso) 5 times, yo, sl 1, k 2 tog, psso, yo, (k 2 tog, yo) 5 times, k 9, rep from * once more, then (yo, sl 1, k 1, psso) 5 times, yo, sl 1, k 2 tog, psso, yo, (k 2 tog, yo) 5 times, k 10, yo, k 1—110 sts. **Rnd 45:** Yo, k 12, * (yo, sl 1, k 1, psso) 5 times, k 1, (k 2 tog, yo) 5 times, k 11, rep from * once more, (yo, sl 1, k 1, psso) 5 times, k 1, (k 2 tog, yo) 5 times, k 12, yo, k 1—112 sts. **Rnd 47:** Yo, k 7, * p and k in the next st, k 6, (yo, sl 1, k 1, psso) 4 times, yo, sl 1, k 2 tog, psso, yo, (k 2 tog, yo) 4 times, k 6, rep from * twice more, p and k in the next st, k 7, yo, k 1—118 sts. **Rnd 49:** Yo, k 7, * k 2 tog, yo, sl 1, k 1, psso, k 6, (yo, sl 1, k 1, psso) 4 times, k 1, (k 2 tog, yo) 4 times, k 6, rep from * twice more, then k 2 tog, yo, sl 1, k 1, psso, k 7, yo, k 1—116 sts. **Rnd 50:** K 9, in next yo, work (k 1, p 1) twice and k 1, * k 31, in the next yo work (k 1, p 1) twice and k 1. Rep from * twice more and then k 10—132 sts. **Rnd 51:** Yo, k 7, * k 2 tog, k 5, sl 1, k 1, psso, k 6, (yo, sl 1, k 1, psso) 3 times, yo, sl 1, k 2 tog, psso, yo, (k 2 tog, yo) 3 times, k 6, rep from * twice more, then k 2 tog, k 5, sl 1, k 1, psso, k 7, yo, k 1—126 sts. **Rnd 53:** Yo, k 7, * k 2 tog, k 2, yo, k 1, yo, k 2, sl 1, k 1, psso, k 6 (yo, sl 1, k 1, psso) 3 times, k 1, (k 2 tog, yo) 3 times, k 6,

rep from * twice more, then k 2 tog, k 2, yo, k 1, yo, k 2, sl 1, k 1, psso, k 7, yo, k 1—128 sts. **Rnd 55:** Yo, k 7, * k 2 tog, k 2, yo, (k 1, yo) 3 times, k 2, sl 1, k 1, psso, k 6, (yo, sl 1, k 1, psso) twice, yo, sl 1, k 2 tog, psso, yo, (k 2 tog, yo) twice, k 6, rep from * twice more, k 2 tog, k 2, yo, (k 1, yo) 3 times, k 2, sl 1, k 1, psso, k 7, yo, k 1—138 sts. **Rnd 57:** Yo, k 7, * k 2 tog, k 11, sl 1, k 1, psso, k 6 (yo, sl 1, k 1, psso) twice, k 1, (k 2 tog, yo) twice, k 6, rep from * twice more, then k 2 tog, k 1, sl 1, k 1, psso, k 7, yo, k 1—132 sts. **Rnd 59:** Yo, k 7, * k 2 tog, k 3, (yo, k 1) 5 times, yo, k 3, sl 1, k 1, psso, k 6, yo, sl 1, k 1, psso, yo, sl 1, k 2 tog, psso, yo, k 2 tog, yo, k 6, rep from * twice more, then k 2 tog, k 3, (yo, k 1) 5 times, yo, k 3, sl 1, k 1, psso, k 7, yo, k 1—150 sts. **Rnd 61:** Yo, k 7, * k 2 tog, k 17, sl 1, k 1, psso, k 6, yo, sl 1, k 1, psso, k 1, k 2 tog, yo, k 6, rep from * twice more, then k 2 tog, k 17, sl 1, k 1, psso, k 7, yo, k 1—144 sts. **Rnd 63:** Yo, k 7, * k 2 tog, k 17, sl 1, k 1, psso, k 6, yo, sl 1, k 2 tog, psso, yo, k 6, rep from * twice more, then k 2 tog, k 17, sl 1, k 1, psso, k 7, yo, k 1—138 sts. **Rnd 65:** Yo, k 7, * k 2 tog, k 5, yo, k 2, yo, (k 1, yo) 3 times, k 2, yo, k 5, sl 1, k 1, psso, k 13, rep from * twice more, then k 2 tog, k 5, yo, k 2, yo, (k 1, yo) 3 times, k 2, yo, k 5, sl 1, k 1, psso, k 7, yo, k 1—156 sts. **Rnd 67:** Yo, k 7, * k 2 tog, k 23, sl 1, k 1, psso, k 11, rep from * twice more, then k 2 tog, k 23, sl 1, k 1, psso, k 7, yo, k 1—150 sts. **Rnd 69:** On 1st needle bind off the next 6 sts (1 st remains on right-hand needle), then * (k 2 tog, sl the 1st st on right-hand needle over the 2nd st of the same needle, make a ch 5) 6 times. *To Make a Ch 5:* (Sl the st remaining on right-hand needle back to the left-hand needle and k it) 5 times, k 3 tog, sl the 1st st on right-hand needle over the 2nd st of the same needle, ch 5, (k 2 tog, sl the 1st st on the right-hand needle over the 2nd st of the same needle, ch 5) 5 times, sl 1, k 1, psso, sl the 1st st on the right-hand needle over the 2nd st of the same needle (1 st remains on the right-hand needle) then including the st on the right-hand needle, bind off 9 sts. Rep from * 3 times more, ending the last repeat with bind off 8 sts—1 st remains on the needle. Place this st onto the next needle and on the 2nd, 3rd, and 4th needles bind off the 1st 7 sts, then starting at * work as for previous needle. Fasten off. Starch piece lightly and press.

MEDALLION
As shown on page 107

Design and directions courtesy of D.M.C. Corporation

Doily measures approximately 18 inches in diameter.

MATERIALS: D.M.C. Crochet Superba, Art.163: 5 balls. 5 10-inch double pointed needles No. 0. Steel crochet hook No. 9.

Cast on 10 sts on 4 needles, 2 on each of 2 needles and 3 on each of the other 2 needles. **Rnds 1, 2, 4, 5, 8, 11, 14, 17, 20, 23, 26, 29, 31, 33, 35, 37, 39, 41, 43, 45, 47, 49, 55:** K. **Rnd 3:** * Yo, k 1, rep from * around. **Rnd 6:** * Yo twice, k 2 tog, rep from * around.

Rnd 7: * K 1, p 1, k 1, rep from * around and end k the 1st st of the 1st needle and sl it onto the 4th needle. **Rnd 9:** * Yo twice, k 3, rep from * around. **Rnds 10, 13:** * K 1, p 1, k 3, rep from * around and end k the 1st st of the 1st needle and sl it onto the 4th needle. **Rnd 12:** * Yo twice, k 1, p 3 tog, k 1, rep from * around. **Rnd 15:** * Yo twice, k 5, rep from * around. **Rnds 16, 19:** * K 1, p 1, k 5, rep from * around and end k the 1st st of the 1st needle and sl it onto the 4th needle. **Rnd 18:** * Yo twice, k 2, p 3 tog, k 2, rep from * around. **Rnd 21:** * Yo twice, k 7, rep from * around. **Rnds 22, 25:** * K 1, p 1, k 7, rep from * around and end k the 1st st of the 1st needle and sl it onto the 4th needle. **Rnd 24:** * Yo twice, k 3, p 3 tog, k 3, rep from * around. **Rnd 27:** * Yo twice, k 9, rep from * around. **Rnd 28:** * K 1, p 1, k 9, rep from * around and end k the 1st st of the 1st needle and sl it onto the 4th needle. **Rnd 30:** * Yo, k 4, p 3 tog, k 4, rep from * around. **Rnd 32:** * Yo, k 1, yo, k 9, rep from * around. **Rnd 34:** * Yo, k 3, yo, k 3, p 3 tog, k 3, rep from * around. **Rnd 36:** * Yo, k 2 tog, yo, k 1, yo, k 1, sl 1, psso, yo, k 7, rep from * around. **Rnd 38:** * Yo, k 2 tog, yo, k 3, yo, sl 1, k 1, psso, yo, k 2, p 3 tog, k 2, rep from * around. **Rnd 40:** * (Yo, k 2 tog) twice, yo, k 1, (yo, sl 1, k 1, psso) twice, yo, k 5, rep from * around. **Rnd 42:** * (Yo, k 2 tog) twice, yo, k 3 (yo, sl 1, k 1, psso) twice, yo, k 1, p 3 tog, k 1, rep from * around. **Rnd 44:** * (Yo, k 2 tog) 3 times, yo, k 1, (yo, sl 1, k 1, psso) 3 times, yo, k 3, rep from * around. **Rnd 46:** * (Yo, k 2 tog) 3 times, yo, k 3, (yo, sl 1, k 1, psso) 3 times, yo, p 3 tog, rep from * around. **Rnd 48:** * (K 2 tog, yo) 3 times, k 5, (yo, sl 1, k 1, psso) 3 times, k 1, rep from * around. **Rnd 50:** K 1 * (yo, k 2 tog) twice, yo, k 3, yo twice, sl 1, k 1, psso, k 2, (yo, sl 1, k 1, psso) twice, yo, sl 1, k 2 tog, psso, rep from * around working the last dec with the 1st st of the 1st needle. **Rnd 51:** K 9, p 1, k 9, rep from * around. **Rnd 52:** * (K 2 tog, yo) twice, k 10, (yo, sl 1, k 1, psso) twice, k 1, rep from * around. **Rnd 53:** K 7, yo twice, k 2 tog, yo twice, sl 1, k 1, psso, yo twice, k 8, rep from * around. **Rnd 54:** K 1 * yo, k 2 tog, yo, k 5, p 1, k 2, p 1, k 2, p 1, k 4, yo, sl 1, k 1, psso, yo, sl 1, k 2 tog, psso, rep from * around working the last dec with the 1st st of the 1st needle. **Rnd 56:** * K 2 tog, yo, k 6, yo twice, k 3, yo twice, k 3, yo twice, k 6, yo, sl 1, k 1, psso, k 1, rep from * around. **Rnd 57:** * K 9, p 1, k 4, p 1, k 4, p 1, k 9, rep from * around. **Rnd 58:** K 1, * yo, k 26, yo, sl 1, k 2 tog, psso, rep from * around, working the last dec with the 1st st of the 1st needle. **Rnd 59:** * K 9, yo twice, k 5, yo twice, k 5, yo twice, k 10, rep from * around. **Rnd 60:** K 1, * k 2 tog, k 7, p 1, k 6, p 1, k 6, p 1, k 6, sl 1, k 1, psso, sl 1, k 2 tog, psso, rep from * around, working the last dec with the 1st st of the 1st needle. **Rnd 61:** K 1, * k 2 tog, k 24, sl 1, k 1, psso, sl 1, k 2 tog, psso, rep from * around, working the last dec with the 1st st of the 1st needle.

Crochet Edging: Sl the last st of Rnd 61 onto a crochet hook, then work * 1 double crochet into each of the next 2 sts, (1 double crochet joining the next 2 sts, chain 5) 3 times, 1 double crochet joining the next 3 sts, (chain 5, 1 double crochet joining the next 2 sts) twice, chain 5, 1 double crochet joining the next 3 sts, (chain 5, 1 double crochet joining the next 2 sts) 3 times, 1 double crochet into each of the next 3 sts, rep from * around and fasten off.

KALEIDOSCOPE
As shown on page 106

Design and directions courtesy of Coats & Clark, Inc.

Doily measures 18½ inches in diameter.

MATERIALS: Clark's Big Ball Mercerized Crochet, Art. B.34 or Art. B.345, size 30: 1 ball. 6 9-inch double-pointed needles No. 0. Steel crochet hook No. 10.

Starting at center, cast on 10 sts. Divide sts among 5 needles, having 2 sts on each needle. Join, being careful not to twist sts. **Rnd 1:** (Yo, k 1) 10 times—20 sts, counting each yo as 1 st. **Rnd 2 and All Even Rnds:** K.

Note: Hereafter work the directions as given once across each of the 5 needles unless otherwise stated.

Rnd 3: K 1, yo, k 2, yo, k 1. **Rnd 5:** K 2, yo, k 3, yo, k 1. **Rnd 7:** K 3, yo, k 4, yo, k 1. **Rnd 9:** K 4, yo, k 5, yo, k 1. **Rnd 11:** K 5, yo, k 6, yo, k 1. **Rnd 13:** K 6, yo, k 7, yo, k 1. **Rnd 15:** K 7, yo, k 8, yo, k 1. **Rnd 19:** K 9, yo, k 10, yo, k 1. **Rnd 21:** K 10, yo, k 11, yo, k 1. **Rnd 22:** (K across needle to within last 2 sts, sl last 2 sts onto next needle) 4 times, k across 5th needle, sl last 2 sts just made onto 1st needle—24 sts on each needle.

Note: Hereafter work directions as given twice across each of the 5 needles unless otherwise stated.

Rnd 23: Yo, k 1, yo, k 11. **Rnd 25:** Yo, k 3, yo, k 4, sl 1, k 2 tog, psso, k 4. **Rnd 27:** Yo, k 5, yo, k 3, sl 1, k 2 tog, psso, k 3. **Rnd 29:** Yo, k 7, yo, k 2, sl 1, k 2 tog, psso, k 2. **Rnd 31:** Yo, k 9, yo, k 1, sl 1, k 2 tog, psso, k 1. **Rnd 33:** Yo, k 5, yo, k 1, yo, k 5, yo, sl 1, k 2 tog, psso. **Rnd 34:** K 32 sts on each needle. Fasten off. Sl the 1st 6 sts of each needle to preceding needle. Attach thread to 1st st on 1st needle. **Rnd 35:** Yo, k 3, yo, k 13—36 sts on each needle. **Rnd 37:** (Yo, k 5) twice, sl 1, k 2 tog, psso, k 5. **Rnd 39:** Yo, k 1, yo, sl 1, k 1, psso, k 1, k 2 tog, yo, k 1, yo, k 4, sl 1, k 2 tog, psso, k 4. **Rnd 41:** Yo, k 3, yo, sl 1, k 2 tog, psso, (yo, k 3) twice, sl 1, k 2 tog, psso, k 3. **Rnd 43:** Yo, k 1, yo, sl 1, k 2 tog, psso, yo, k 3, yo, sl 1, k 2 tog, psso, yo, k 1, yo, k 2, sl 1, k 2 tog, psso, k 2. **Rnd 45:** Yo, k 3, yo, k 7, yo, k 3, yo, k 1, sl 1, k 2 tog, psso, k 1 —40 sts on each needle. **Rnd 47:** Yo, k 1, yo, sl 1, k 2 tog, psso, yo, k 9, yo, sl 1, k 2 tog, psso, yo, k 1, yo, sl 1, k 2 tog, psso. **Rnd 49:** Yo, k 3, yo, k 2, sl 1, k 1, psso, k 5, k 2 tog, k 2, yo, k 3, yo, k 1—44 sts on each needle. **Rnd 50:** Rep Rnd 22 on 44 sts on each needle. **Rnd 51:** K 3, yo, sl 1, k 2 tog, psso, yo, k 1, yo, k 2, sl 1, k 1, psso, k 3, k 2 tog, k 2, yo, k 1, yo, sl 1, k 2 tog, psso, yo. **Rnd 53:** Yo, k 3, yo, sl 1, k 1, psso, yo, k 3,

yo, k 2, sl 1, k 1, psso, k 1, k 2 tog, k 2, yo, k 3, yo, k 2 tog—48 sts on each needle. **Rnd 55:** Yo, k 5, yo, sl 1, k 1, psso, yo, k 4, yo, k 2, sl 1, k 2 tog, psso, k 2, yo, k 4, yo, k 2 tog—52 sts on each needle. **Rnd 57:** Yo, k 7, yo, sl 1, k 1, psso, yo, k 15, yo, k 2 tog—56 sts on each needle. **Rnd 59:** Yo, k 2, k 2 tog, yo, k 1, yo, sl 1, k 1, psso, k 2, yo, sl 1, k 1, psso, yo, k 2, sl 1, k 1 psso, k 7, k 2 tog, k 2, yo, k 2 tog. **Rnd 61:** Yo, k 2, k 2 tog, yo, k 3, yo, sl 1, k 1, psso, k 2, yo, sl 1, k 1, psso, yo, k 2, sl 1, k 1, psso, k 5, k 2 tog, k 2, yo, k 2 tog. **Rnd 63:** Yo, k 2, k 2 tog, yo, k 5, yo, sl 1, k 1, psso, k 2, yo, sl 1, k 1, psso, yo, k 2, sl 1, k 1, psso, k 3, k 2 tog, k 2, yo, k 2 tog. **Rnd 65:** Yo, k 2, k 2 tog, yo, k 7, yo, sl 1, k 1, psso, k 2, yo, sl 1, k 1, psso, yo, k 2, sl 1, k 1, psso, k 1, k 2 tog, k 2, yo, k 2 tog. **Rnd 67:** Yo, k 2, k 2 tog, yo, k 4, yo, k 1, yo, k 4, yo, sl 1, k 1, psso, k 2, yo, sl 1, k 1, psso, yo, k 2, sl 1, k 2 tog, psso, k 2, yo, k 2 tog— 60 sts on each needle. **Rnd 69:** Yo, k 2, k 2 tog, yo, k 3, k 2 tog, yo, k 3, yo, sl 1, k 1, psso, k 3, yo, sl 1, k 1, psso, k 2, yo, sl 1, k 1, psso, yo, k 1, sl 1, k 2 tog, psso, k 1, yo, k 2 tog. **Rnd 71:** Yo, k 2, k 2 tog, yo, k 3, k 2 tog, yo, k 5, yo, sl 1, k 1, psso, k 3, yo, sl 1, k 1, psso, k 2, yo, sl 1, k 1, psso, yo, sl 1, k 2 tog, psso, yo, k 2 tog. **Rnd 73:** Yo, k 2, k 2 tog, yo, k 3, k 2 tog, yo, k 1, yo, sl 1, k 1, psso, k 1, k 2 tog, yo, k 1, yo, sl 1, k 1, psso, k 3, yo, sl 1, k 1, psso, k 2, yo, sl 1, k 1, psso, k 1, k 2 tog. **Rnd 75:** Yo, k 2, k 2 tog, yo, k 3, k 2 tog, yo, k 3, yo, sl 1, k 2 tog, psso, yo, k 3, yo, sl 1, k 1, psso, k 3, yo,

sl 1, k 1, psso, k 2, yo, sl 1, k 2 tog, psso.
Rnd 76: K 60 sts on each needle. Fasten off.

Sl the 1st 9 sts of each needle to preceding needle. Attach thread as before. **Rnd 77:** Yo, k 1, yo, sl 1, k 2 tog, psso, yo, k 3, yo, sl 1, k 2 tog, psso, yo, k 1, yo, sl 1, k 1, psso, k 3, yo, sl 1, k 1, psso, k 5, k 2 tog, yo, k 3, k 2 tog. **Rnd 79:** Yo, k 3, yo, k 1, yo, sl 1, k 1, psso, k 1, k 2 tog, yo, k 1, yo, k 3, yo, sl 1, k 1, psso, k 3, yo, sl 1, k 1, psso, k 3, k 2 tog, yo, k 3, k 2 tog—64 sts on each needle. **Rnd 81:** Yo, k 1, (yo, sl 1, k 2 tog, psso, yo, k 3) twice, yo, sl 1, k 2 tog, psso, yo, k 1, yo, sl 1, k 1, psso, k 3, yo, sl 1, k 1, psso, k 1, k 2 tog, yo, k 3, k 2 tog. **Rnd 83:** Yo, k 3, yo, k 1, (yo, sl 1, k 1, psso, k 1, k 2 tog, yo, k 1) twice, yo, k 3, yo, sl 1, k 1, psso, k 3, yo, sl 1, k 2 tog, psso, yo, k 3, k 2 tog—68 sts on each needle. **Rnd 85:** Yo, k 1, (yo, sl 1, k 2 tog, psso, yo, k 3) 3 times, yo, sl 1, k 2 tog, psso, yo, k 1, yo, sl 1, k 1, psso, k 7, k 2 tog. **Rnd 87:** Yo, k 3, (yo, k 1, yo, sl 1, k 1, psso, k 1, k 2 tog) 3 times, yo, k 1, yo, k 3, yo, sl 1, k 1, psso, k 5, k 2 tog—72 sts on each needle. **Rnd 89:** Yo, k 1, (yo, sl 1, k 2 tog, psso, yo, k 3) 4 times, yo, sl 1, k 2 tog, psso, yo, k 1, yo, sl 1, k 1, psso, k 3, k 2 tog. **Rnd 91:** Yo, k 3, (yo, k 1, yo, sl 1, k 1, psso, k 1, k 2 tog) 4 times, yo, k 1, yo, k 3, yo, sl 1, k 1, psso, k 1, k 2 tog—76 sts on each needle. **Rnd 93:** Yo, k 2 tog, k 2 (yo, sl 1, k 2 tog, psso, yo, k 3) 4 times, yo, sl 1, k 2 tog, psso, yo, k 2, k 2 tog, yo, sl 1, k 2 tog, psso—72 sts on each needle. **Rnd 95:** Sl 1st st on 1st needle onto 5th needle, insert

crochet hk through 1st 3 sts on 1st needle as if to k, thread over and draw lp through the 3 sts, drop these 3 sts off needle (cluster made), ch 6, * make a cluster over the next 3 sts on needle, ch 6. Rep from * around. Join with a sl st to tip of 1st cluster. Fasten off. Starch lightly and press.

LILY POND
As shown on page 111

Design and directions courtesy of Coats & Clark, Inc.

Each motif measures 9 inches across center. Single-size spread measures 76 x 116 inches; double, 90 x 116 inches.

MATERIALS: J. & P. Coats Knit-Cro-Sheen Art. A.64: 46 balls of white, ecru, or cream, or 70 balls of any other color for single-size spread; 59 balls of white, ecru, or cream, or 83 balls of any other color for double-size spread. 1 set of 4 double-pointed needles No. 1. Straight knitting needles No. 1.

Motif (Make 160 for single-size spread, 189 for double-size spread): Starting at center and using double-pointed needles, cast on 12 sts. Divide sts among 3 needles, having 4 sts on each needle, then join, being careful not to twist sts.

Note: The sts for 2 sections of the design are on each needle—6 sections in all. **Rnds 1, 2:** P.

From this point on, work the directions as given twice across each of the 3 needles, unless otherwise stated. The number of sts on each needle is given at end of each rnd.

Rnd 3: K 1, yo, k 1—6 sts, counting each yo as 1 st. **Rnd 4:** P. **Rnd 5:** (K 1, yo) twice, k 1—10 sts. **Rnd 6:** P. **Rnd 7:** (K 1, yo) 4 times, k 1—18 sts. **Rnd 8:** P 2, k 5, p 2. **Rnd 9:** K 1, yo, sl 1, k 1, psso, (k 1, yo) twice, k 1, k 2 tog, yo, k 1—22 sts. **Rnd 10:** P 2, k 7, p 2. **Rnd 11:** (K 1, yo, k 4, yo) twice, k 1—30 sts. **Rnd 12:** P 3, k 9, p 3. **Rnd 13:** (K 1, yo, k 6, yo) twice, k 1—38 sts. **Rnd 14:** P 4, k 11, p 4. **Rnd 15:** K 1, yo, sl 1, k 1, psso, k 1, sl 1, k 1, psso, k 7, k 2 tog, k 1, k 2 tog, yo, k 1—34 sts. **Rnd 16:** P 4, k 9, p 4. **Rnd 17:** K 1, yo, k 3, sl 1, k 1, psso, k 5, k 2 tog, k 3, yo, k 1. **Rnd 18:** P 5, k 7, p 5. **Rnd 19:** K 1, yo, k 4, sl 1, k 1, psso, k 3, k 2 tog, k 4, yo, k 1. **Rnd 20:** P 6, k 5, p 6. **Rnd 21:** K 1, yo, sl 1, k 1, psso, k 3, sl 1, k 1, psso, k 1, k 2 tog, k 3, k 2 tog, yo, k 1—30 sts. **Rnd 22:** P 6, k 3, p 6. **Rnd 23:** K 1, yo, k 5, sl 1, k 2 tog, psso, k 5, yo, k 1. **Rnd 24:** P 15, place a marker on needle separating the 2 sections on the needle, p 15.

From this point on the number of sts is given for each section of the design. Be sure to always slip markers on each rnd.

Rnd 25: * K 1, yo, k across to within last st of this section, yo, k 1. Rep from * across each section on each needle. **Rnd 26:** P. **Rnds 27, 28:** Rep Rnds 25 and 26—19 sts. **Rnd 29:** ** K 1, yo, k 1, * yo, k 2 tog, rep from * across to within last st of this section, yo, k 1, then rep from ** across each section on each needle. **Rnd 30:** ** P 2, * k 1, p 1, rep from * to within last st of this section, p 1, then rep from ** across each section on each needle. **Rnds 31–38:** Rep Rnds 29 and 30 alternately 4 times—29 sts at end of

Rnd 38. **Rnds 39–46:** Rep Rnds 25 and 26 alternately 4 times—37 sts at end of Rnd 46. Bind off.

Half Motif (Make 10 for single-size spread; 12 for double): Starting at long edge and using straight needles, cast on 79 sts. **Row 1:** K. **Rows 2–8:** K 2 tog, k across to within last 2 sts, k 2 tog—65 sts at end of Row 8. **Row 9:** Bind off 19 sts, place the 1 st remaining on the right-hand needle back onto the left-hand needle, * k 1, yo, sl 1, k 1, psso, (k 1, yo) twice, k 1, k 2 tog, yo, k 1, rep from * twice more and then k remaining 19 sts—52 sts. **Row 10:** Bind off 19 sts, place the 1 st remaining on the right-hand needle back onto the left-hand needle, * k 2, p 7, k 2, rep from * across— 33 sts. **Row 11:** * (K 1, yo, k 4, yo) twice, k 1, rep from * across—45 sts. **Row 12:** * K 3, p 9, k 3, rep from * across. **Row 13:** * (K 1, yo, k 6, yo) twice, k 1, rep from * across— 57 sts. **Row 14:** * K 4, p 11, k 4, rep from * across. **Row 15:** * K 1, yo, sl 1, k 1, psso, k 1, sl 1, k 1, psso, k 7, k 2 tog, k 1, k 2 tog, yo, k 1, rep from * across—51 sts. **Row 16:** * K 4, p 9, k 4, rep from * across. **Row 17:** * K 1, yo, k 3, sl 1, k 1, psso, k 5, k 2 tog, k 3, yo, k 1, rep from * across. **Row 18:** * K 5, p 7, k 5, rep from * across. **Row 19:** * K 1, yo, k 4, sl 1, k 1, psso, k 3, k 2 tog, k 4, yo, k 1, rep from * across. **Row 20:** * K 6, p 5, k 6, rep from * across. **Row 21:** * K 1, yo, sl 1, k 1, psso, k 3, sl 1, k 1, psso, k 1, k 2 tog, k 3, k 2 tog, yo, k 1, rep from

* across—45 sts. **Row 22:** * K 6, p 3, k 6, rep from * across. **Row 23:** * K 1, yo, k 5, sl 1, k 2 tog, psso, k 5, yo, k 1, rep from * across. **Row 24:** (K 15, place a marker on needle) twice, k 15. Remember to slip markers when they appear. **Row 25:** (K 1, yo, k across to within 1 st before marker, yo, k 1) twice, k 1, yo, k across to within last st, yo, k 1. **Row 26:** K. **Rows 27, 28:** Rep Rows 25 and 26—57 sts. **Row 29:** * K 1, yo, k 1, ** yo, k 2 tog, rep from ** across to within 1 st before marker, yo, k 1, rep from * once more then k 1, yo, k 1, *** yo, k 2 tog, rep from *** across to within last st, yo, k 1. **Row 30:** * K 2, ** p 1, k 1, rep from ** across to within 1 st before marker, k 1, rep from * once more, k 2, *** p 1, k 1, rep from *** across to within last st, k 1. **Rows 31–38:** Rep Rows 29 and 30 alternately 4 times—87 sts at end of Row 38. **Rows 39–46:** Rep Rows 25 and 26 alternately 4 times —111 sts at the end of Row 46. Bind off. Sew the 19 bound-off sts on each end of long edge to corresponding end-of-row edges, thus completing the half motif. Sew motifs and half motifs neatly together having the straight edges of the motifs at top and bottom of each vertical joining and arranging them so that each alternate vertical row of motifs is set midway between the motifs at either side of it. Sew the half motifs in place along the top and bottom edges of the completed bedspread between the motifs at those edges, giving in this way a straight edge along the top and bottom and a pointed edge along the sides. Starch finished piece lightly and press.

LACE DIAMONDS

As shown on page 111

Design and directions courtesy of Brunswick Worsted Mills Inc.

Carriage throw measures 39 x 45 inches without edging.

MATERIALS: Brunswick Baby Zephyr or Windspun: 11 1-ounce skeins. 29-inch circular knitting needle, No. 5. Aluminium crochet hook No. C.

GAUGE: 6 sts and 9 rows = 1 inch

PATTERN STITCH:

Row 1: K 4, * K 3 tog, yo, k 8, rep from * across and end last rep with k 5 instead of k 8.
Row 2 and All Wrong-Side Rows: P.
Row 3: K 3, * k 2 tog, yo, k 1, yo, sl 1, k 1, psso, k 5, rep from * across and end last rep with k 3 instead of k 5.
Row 5: K 2, * k 2 tog, yo, k 3, yo, sl 1, k 1, psso, k 3, rep from * across and end last rep with k 2 instead of k 3.
Row 7: K 1, * k 2 tog, yo, k 1, yo, sl 1, k 2 tog, psso, yo, k 1, yo, sl 1, k 1, psso, k 1, rep from * across.
Row 9: K 2 tog, * yo, k 7, yo, sl 1, k 2 tog, psso, rep from * across and end last rep with sl 1, k 1, psso, instead of sl 1, k 2 tog, psso.
Row 11: K 2, * yo, sl 1, k 2 tog, psso, yo, k 1, yo, sl 1, k 2 tog, psso, yo, k 3, rep from *

across and end last rep with k 2 instead
of k 3.

Row 13: K 2, * k 2 tog, yo, k 3, yo, sl 1,
k 1, psso, k 3, rep from * across and end
with k 2 instead of k 3.

Row 15: K 4, * yo, sl 1, k 2 tog, psso, yo,
k 7, rep from * across and end with k 4
instead of k 7.

Row 16: P.

Repeat Rows 1 through 16 for pattern
stitch.

Cast on 231 sts and rep pattern st 22
times, or until piece measures desired length,
ending with Row 16 of pattern. Bind off.

Crochet Edging: Attach yarn at corner and
work 1 row of single crochet (sc) around the
entire outer edge of the finished piece,
spacing the sc about 10 sts to each pattern.
Sl st to join at the end of the rnd. **Rnd 2:**
Chain (ch) 3, * double crochet (dc) in each
of the next 3 sts, ch 1, skip 1 st, rep from
* around working (dc, ch 3 and dc) in each
corner st. Sl st to join. **Rnd 3:** * Ch 5, sc
between every 2nd and 3rd dc of the previous
rnd and rep from * around, adjusting sts at
corners so that the sc will fall in the center
of the corner sts. **Rnd 4:** * Dc 8 times in the
1st space (sp), sc in the next sp, rep from *
around to start of rnd, adjusting sts at last
corner so that work lays flat. **Rnd 5:** * Dc in
the 1st dc of the previous scallop, ch 3, sc
in the same dc (picot), rep dc and picot
across 7 dc, working a dc without picot in
the 8th dc, sc in sp, then rep from * around
to beginning. Fasten off. Block piece into
shape.

WHISPER

As shown on page 122

*Design and directions courtesy of Reynolds Yarns,
Inc.*

*Directions for shell are written for size 10. Changes
for sizes 12, 14, 16, 18 are in parentheses.*

**MATERIALS: Reynolds Parfait: 5 (5, 6, 6, 7) 1-
ounce balls. Straight knitting needles No. 4 and
No. 5.**

*GAUGE: 11 sts = 2 inches, 7 rows = 1 inch on
No. 5 needles*

PATTERN STITCH:

Row 1 (Right Side): K 2 (2, 2, 1, 1), * yo,
k 1, yo, k 2 tog, k 1, k 2 tog, rep from *
across and end k 2 (2, 2, 1, 1).

Rows 2, 4, 6: P.

Row 3: K 2 (2, 2, 1, 1), * yo, k 3, yo, k 3
tog, rep from * across and end k 2 (2, 2, 1, 1).

Row 5: K 2 (2, 2, 1, 1), * k 2 tog, k 1, k 2
tog, yo, k 1, yo, rep from * across and end
yo, k 2 (2, 2, 1, 1).

Row 7: K 2 (2, 2, 1, 1), * k 3 tog, yo, k 3,
yo, rep from * across and end yo, k 2
(2, 2, 1, 1).

Row 8: P.

Repeat these 8 rows for pattern stitch.

Back: With No. 4 needles cast on 94 (100,
106, 110, 116) sts. Work in stockinette st
for 7 rows, ending with a k row. K next
row on wrong side for hemline. Work 6
more rows in stockinette st, ending with a p
row. Change to No. 5 needles. Work in
pattern st until piece measures 12½ inches
above hemline, or desired length to under-

arms. Mark last row. *Shape Armholes:*
Being sure to maintain pattern, bind off 5
(6, 8, 8, 9) sts at beg of each of the next 2
rows, then dec 1 st at beg and end of every
other row 3 (4, 4, 4, 5) times. Work even
now on 78 (80, 82, 86, 88) sts until armholes
measure 6 (6, 6½, 6½, 7) inches above
the marked row. *Shape Neck:* Work across
19 (20, 21, 22, 23) sts, sl the next 40 (40,
40, 42, 42) sts onto a holder, attach another
ball of yarn and work across the remaining
19 (20, 21, 22, 23) sts. Working on both
sides at the same time, dec 1 st at each
neck edge every row 10 times, then work
even until armholes measure 7½ (7½, 8,
8, 8½) inches above the marked row.
Shape Shoulders: Bind off 3 sts at each
armhole edge every other row twice, then
3 (4, 5, 6, 7) sts once.

Front: Work same as back.

Finishing: Sew right shoulder seam.
Neckband: With No. 4 needles and starting
at left shoulder of front and working on
right side of piece, pick up and k 132 sts
around the neck edge, including the sts
on holders. Starting with a p row, work
in stockinette st for 6 rows, then k the
next row on the wrong side of work for
hemline, then starting with a k row, work
in stockinette st for 6 more rows. Bind off
loosely. Sew left shoulder seam. *Armhole
Bands:* With No. 4 needles and starting at
underarm, pick up 88 (88, 92, 92, 96) sts
around the armhole edge. Work in same
manner as for neckband. Bind off. Sew side

seams. Turn all hems to wrong side of
work at hemlines and sew in place. Steam
finished piece lightly.

TEARDROPS
As shown on page 120

*Design and directions courtesy of William Unger &
Co., Inc.*

*Directions for shell are written for size 10. Changes
for sizes 12, 14, 16 are in parentheses.*

**MATERIALS: Unger's Iris: 3 (4, 4, 5) 1½-ounce
balls. Straight knitting needles No. 3 and No. 4.**

*GAUGE: 5 teardrops = 4½ inches on No. 4
needles*

Note: When working the pattern, the actual
stitch count occurs on Rows 8 and 16. Be
careful when shaping that you allow for
the increase of the teardrops and that you
come back to the number of sts called
for. In this pattern, 8 rows form 1 teardrop
band.

PATTERN STITCH:

Row 1: P 1, * in the next st work k 1, p 1,
k 1, p 1, k 1 (teardrop), p 3, rep from *
across.
Rows 2, 4: * K 3, p 5, rep from * across
and end k 1.
Row 3: P 1, * k 5, p 3, rep from * across.
Row 5: P 1, * sl 1, k 1, psso, k 1, k 2 tog,
p 3, rep from * across.
Row 6: * K 3, p 3, rep from * across and
end k 1.

Row 7: P 1, * k 3 tog, p 3, rep from * across.

Row 8: K.

Row 9: * P 3, work a teardrop in next st, rep from * across and end p 1.

Rows 10, 12: K 1, * p 5, k 3, rep from * across.

Row 11: * P 3, k 5, rep from * across and end p 1.

Row 13: * P 3, sl 1, k 1, psso, k 1, k 2 tog, rep from * across and end p 1.

Row 14: K 1, * P 3, k 3, rep from * across.

Row 15: * P 3, k 3 tog, rep from * across and end p 1.

Row 16: K.

Repeat these 16 rows for pattern stitch.

Back: With No. 4 needles, cast on 77 (81, 85, 89) sts. K 1 row. Change to No. 3 needles and pattern st and work even until 6 teardrop bands have been completed. Change to No. 4 needles and continue in pattern until you have worked the last k row of the 11th teardrop band. *Shape Armholes:* **Row 1:** Bnd off 7 sts, k to end of row. **Row 2:** Bind off 7 sts, work until there are 4 p sts on the needle, work in pattern to within the last 6 sts, p 6, k 2 tog at beg and end of the next row, then at beg and end of every other row 3 times more—55 (59, 63, 67) sts. Work even now to within the last row of the 4th (4th, 5th, 5th) teardrop band above the armhole shaping, then *Shape Neck:* K 15 (15, 19, 19) sts, sl these sts onto a holder, bind off loosely the next 25 (29,

25, 29) sts then work the remaining 15 (15, 19, 19) sts. Work even now to the last row of the 7th (7th, 8th, 8th) teardrop band above the armhole shaping. Bind off. Place sts from the holder onto a needle, attach the yarn again at the neck edge, and work the other side to correspond.

Front: Work same as back, shaping the neck on the last row of the 2nd (2nd, 3rd, 3rd) teardrop band above the armhole shaping.

Finishing: Back Neck Ribbing: With No. 3 needles and working on right side of piece, pick up and k 69 (73, 73, 77) sts around the neck including the 3 sts on the holder. Work in k 1, p 1, ribbing for 3 rows. Bind off loosely in ribbing. *Fronk Neck Ribbing:* Work same as for back neck ribbing, picking up 103 (107, 107, 111) sts around the neck. Sew shoulder seams. *Armhole Ribbing:* With No. 3 needles and right side of work facing, pick up and k 115 (115, 121, 121) sts around the armholes. Work in ribbing as for the neck. Sew side seams. Steam finished piece lightly on the wrong side.

CHANTILLY
As shown on page 121

Design and directions courtesy of Reynolds Yarns, Inc.

Directions for shell are written for size 10. Changes for sizes 12, 14, 16, 18 are in parentheses.

MATERIALS: Reynolds Parfait: 5 (5, 6, 6, 7) 2-ounce balls. Straight knitting needles No. 5. Steel crochet hook No. 3.

GAUGE: 5 sts and 8 rows = 1 inch.

PATTERN STITCH:

Row 1 (Right Side): P.
Rows 2, 3: K 1, * yo, k 2 tog, rep from * across.
Rows 4, 5: K.
Row 6: P.
Repeat these 6 rows for pattern stitch.

Back: Cast on 87 (89, 95, 99, 105) sts. Work in pattern until piece measures 12½ inches from start or desired length to underarms. Mark last row. Shape Armholes: Being careful to maintain pattern, bind off 5 (5, 6, 6, 7) sts at beg of each of the next 2 rows, then dec 1 st at beg and end of every other row 3 (3, 4, 5, 6) times. Work even now on 71 (73, 75, 77, 79) sts until armholes measure 6¼ (6½, 6¾, 7, 7¼) inches above the marked row. Shape Neck and Shoulders: Work across 17 (18, 19, 20, 21) sts, join another ball of yarn, bind off the center 37 sts, then work to end of row. Working on both sides at same time, dec 1 st at each neck edge every row 6 times and at same time, when armhole measures 7¼ (7½, 7¾, 8, 8¼) inches above the marked row, bind off 4 sts at each armhole edge every other row twice, then 3 (4, 5, 6, 7) sts once.

Front: Work same as back.

Finishing: Sew side and shoulder seams.
Crochet Edging: Rnd 1: With right side of work facing, work 1 row of single crochet (sc) along the lower edge of your garment, spacing the sts so that work lays flat. Join with a sl st and chain (ch) 1.
Rnd 2: * Work 1 sc in each of 3 sts, ch 4, 1 sl st in same st as last sc (picot), rep from * around, then join with a sl st and fasten off. Work 2 rnds of the crochet border in the same manner around the armholes and neck edge. Block piece lightly.

CHAMPAGNE
As shown on page 122

Design and directions courtesy of Reynolds Yarns, Inc.

Directions for shell are written for size 10. Changes for sizes 12, 14, 16, 18 are in parentheses.

MATERIALS: Reynolds Mohair No. 1: 3 (3, 4, 4, 5) 50-gram balls. Straight knitting needles No. 7.

GAUGE: 4 pattern sts and 6 rows = 1 inch.

Note: In working the pattern st, always sl st as if to purl.

PATTERN STITCH:

Row 1 (Right Side): K 1 (2, 4, 1, 3), * yo, k 3, sl 1, k 2 tog, psso the k 2 tog, k 3, yo, k 1, rep from * across and end last rep with k 1 (2, 4, 1, 3).
Rows 2, 4: P.
Row 3: K 2 (3, 5, 2, 4), * yo, k 2, sl 1,

k 2 tog, psso the k 2 tog, k 2, yo, k 3, rep from * across and end last rep with k 2 (3, 5, 2, 4).

Row 5: K 0 (1, 3, 0, 2), k 2 tog, * yo, k 1, yo, k 1, sl 1, k 2 tog, psso the k 2 tog, k 1, yo, k 1, yo, sl 1, k 2 tog, psso the k 2 tog, rep from * across and end last rep with yo, sl 1, k 1, psso, k 0 (1, 3, 0, 2).

Row 6: P.

Repeat these 6 rows for pattern stitch.

Back: Cast on 71 (73, 77, 81, 85) sts. Work in stockinette st for 4 rows, ending with a p row. P the next row for hemline. Work in pattern now until piece measures 12½ inches above the hemline or desired length to underarms. Mark the last row. *Shape Armholes:* Being careful to maintain pattern, bind off 4 (4, 5, 6, 7) sts at beg of each of the next 2 rows. Dec 1 st now at beg and end of every other row 3 times, then work even on 57 (59, 61, 63, 65) sts until armholes measure 5½ (5½, 6, 6, 6½) inches above the marked row. *Shape Neck:* Work across 13 (14, 15, 16, 17) sts, sl the center 31 sts onto a holder, join another ball of yarn and work across the remaining 13 (14, 15, 16, 17) sts. Working on both sides at the same time dec 1 st at each neck edge every other row 5 times, then work even until armholes measure 7½ (7½, 8, 8, 8½) inches above the marked row. *Shape Shoulders:* Bind off remaining 8 (9, 10, 11, 12) sts at each armhole edge.

Front: Work same as back.

Finishing: Sew right shoulder seam. *Neckband:* Starting at left shoulder of front and working on right side of piece, pick up and k 96 (100, 104, 108, 112) sts around the neck edge, including the sts on holders. Work in stockinette st for 4 rows, ending with a p row. Bind off loosely. Sew left shoulder seam. *Armhole Bands:* Starting at underarm, and working on right side, pick up and k 72 (76, 80, 84, 88) sts around each armhole edge. Work in same manner as neckband. Bind off loosely. Sew side seams. Turn hem at lower edge in half to wrong side of work and sew in place. The purl rows will be on the right side of the work. Roll the neck and armhole bands in half to the wrong side and sew in place. Steam finished piece lightly.

CANDY CANE
As shown on page 123

Design and directions courtesy of Emile Bernat & Sons Company

Directions for slipover are written for small size (8–10). Changes for medium (12–14) and large (16–18) are in parentheses.

MATERIALS: Bernat Cott'n Silk: 4 (4, 5) 50-gram balls main color and 5 (5, 6) balls contrast color. Straight knitting needles No. 3 and No. 5. Steel crochet hook No. 00. Small button.

GAUGE: 6 sts and 8 rows = 1 inch

PATTERN STITCH:

Row 1: K 2 tog, k 3, * yo, k 1, yo, k 3,

sl 1, k 2 tog, psso, k 3, rep from * across and end yo, k 1, yo, k 3, sl 1, k 1, psso.

Row 2 and All Even Rows: P.

Row 3: K 2 tog, k 2, * yo, k 3, yo, k 2 ,sl 1, k 2 tog, psso, k 2, rep from * across and end yo, k 3, yo, k 2, sl 1, k 1, psso.

Row 5: K 2 tog, k 1, * yo, k 5, yo, k 1, sl 1, k 2 tog, psso, k 1, rep from * across and end yo, k 5, yo, k 1, sl 1, k 1, psso.

Row 7: K 2 tog, * yo, k 7, yo, sl 1, k 2 tog, psso, rep from * across and end yo, k 7, yo, sl 1, k 1, psso.

Row 8: P.

Repeat these 8 rows for pattern stitch.

Striping Pattern: Work in pattern st as follows: * 8 rows contrast color, 8 rows main color, rep from * for striping pattern.

Back: With No. 5 needles and contrast color, cast on 101 (111, 121) sts. P 1 row, then work in striping pattern until piece measures 11 inches. *Shape Armholes:* Bind off 5 sts at beg of each of the next 2 rows, then dec 1 st at beg and end of every other row 5 times. Work even in striping pattern on 81 (91, 101) sts until armholes measure 3¼ (3¾, 4¼) inches, ending with a right side row. *Back Opening:* Continuing in pattern, p 40 (45, 50) sts, join another ball of yarn, bind off center st, then p to end of row. Being careful to maintain pattern, work even on both sides at same time until armholes measure 7¼ (7¾, 8¼) inches. *Shape Shoulders:* Bind off 8 (9, 10) sts 3 times at each arm edge,

sl remaining 16 (18, 20) sts of each side onto a holder.

Front: Work to correspond to back, omitting the back opening until the armholes measure 5¼ (5¾, 6¼) inches ending with a right side row—81 (91, 101) sts. *Shape Neck:* P 30 (33, 36) sts, sl center 21 (25, 29) sts onto a holder, join another ball of yarn and p across remaining sts. Working on both sides at the same time, dec 1 st at each neck edge every other row 6 times, then work even on 24 (27, 30) sts of each side until armholes measure 7¼ (7¾, 8¼) inches. *Shape Shoulders:* Bind off 8 (9, 10) sts at each arm edge 3 times.

Sleeves: With No. 5 needles and contrast color, cast on 71 (81, 91) sts. P 1 row, then work even in striping pattern until piece measures 15 inches, ending with the same row of striping pattern as on back at underarm. *Shape Cap:* Bind off 5 sts at beg of each of the next 2 rows, then dec 1 st at beg and end of every other row for 4¼ (4¾, 5¼) inches. Bind off 3 (4, 5) sts at beg of each of the next 6 rows, then bind off remaining sts.

Finishing: Sew side, shoulder and sleeve seams. Sew in sleeves. *Neckband:* With No. 3 needles and contrast color and working on right side of work, pick up and k 95 (99, 103) sts around neck, including the sts from holders. K 1, p 1 in ribbing

for 2 inches. Bind off loosely in ribbing.
Fold neckband in half and hem. Using
contrast color, work 1 row of single
crochet around the back opening, forming
a buttonloop at the left back neck edge.
Sew on button to correspond to buttonloop.
Steam piece lightly.

MONIQUE
As shown on page 125

Design and directions courtesy of Reynolds Yarns, Inc.

Directions for cardigan are written for small size (10–12). Changes for medium (14–16) and large (18–20) are in parentheses.

MATERIALS: Reynolds Mohair No. 1: 8 (9, 10) 50-gram balls. Straight knitting needles No. 8. Steel crochet hook No. 2. 7 buttons, 1½ yards grosgrain ribbon, net lining for scarf.

GAUGE: 9 pattern stitches = 2 inches; 6 rows = 1 inch

PATTERN STITCH:

Row 1 (Right Side): P 1, k 1 in ribbing on 5 (7, 7) sts, * k 2 tog, yo, k 2 (lace panel), then p 1, k 1 in ribbing on 5 (7, 7) sts and rep from * across.
Row 2: K 1, p 1 in ribbing on 5 (7, 7) sts, * p 2 tog, yo, p 2 (lace panel), then k 1, p 1 in ribbing on 5 (7, 7) sts and rep from * across.

Repeat these 2 rows for pattern stitch.
Note: When shaping this garment, work the broken lace panel at sides in ribbing until there are enough sts to work a complete lace panel.

Back: Cast on 77 (84, 95) sts. Work even in pattern st for 15 (15½, 16) inches or desired length to underarms ending on wrong side of work. Mark the last row. *Shape Armholes:* Being careful to maintain pattern, bind off 4 (4, 5) sts at beg of each of the next 2 rows, then dec 1 st at beg and end of every other row 3 (4, 6) times. Working 7 (10, 7) ribbing sts (instead of broken lace panel) at armhole edges now, work even on 63 (68, 73) sts until armholes measure 7½ (8, 8½) inches above the marked row. *Shape Shoulders:* Bind off loosely 5 sts at beg of each of the next 4 rows, then 5 (6, 7) sts at beg of each of the next 4 rows. Bind off loosely the remaining 23 (24, 25) sts for back of neck.

Left Front: Cast on 43 (51, 53) sts. **Row 1** (Right Side): Work Row 1 of pattern across the row and end the last repeat with 7 (7, 9) ribbing sts for the border. **Row 2:** Work k 1, p 1 ribbing on 7 (7, 9) sts for the border, then work Row 2 of pattern. Continue in this manner now until the piece measures same length as back to underarm. Mark last row. *Shape Armhole:* Bind off 4 (4, 5) sts at armhole edge once, then dec 1 st at the same edge every other row 3 (6, 5) times—36 (41, 43) sts. Continuing to work 7 (8, 8) sts in ribbing at the armhole edge, work even now until the armhole measures 5½ (6, 6½) inches above the marked row. *Shape Neck:* At front edge bind off 10 sts, then complete row. Dec 1 st at same edge every row 6 (9, 9) times—20 (22, 24) sts. Work even now on these sts until armhole measures same as back to shoulder. *Shape Shoulder:* Bind off 5 (6, 7) sts at beg of armhole edge twice. Mark position for 6 buttons evenly spaced along the front edge, placing the 1st one 1 inch from the lower edge and the last one ¾ inch below the neck edge.

Right Front: Cast on 43 (51, 53) sts. **Row 1** (Right Side): Work p 1, k 1 ribbing on 1st 7 (7, 9) sts for the border, then starting at 1st * work Row 1 of pattern to end of row. **Row 2:** Work Row 2 of pattern across and end last rep with ribbing on 7 (7, 9) sts for border. Continue to work in this manner, completing left front to correspond to right front, working in buttonholes opposite markers. *Buttonholes:* Working in ribbing, work 3 sts at beg of front edge, bind off the next 4 sts, then complete the row. On the next row cast on 4 sts over the bound-off sts of previous row.

Sleeves: Cast on 41 (40, 40) sts. Work in pattern as for back for 2 inches. Inc 1 st at beg and end of next row, then rep this inc every 1¼ (1, 1) inches 8 (11, 13) times— 59 (64, 68) sts. Work even now on these sts until the total length is 17½ (18, 18½) inches, or 1 inch more (hem allowance) than the desired length to underarms. *Shape Cap:* Bind off 4 (4, 5) sts at beg of each of the next 2 rows, then dec 1 st at beg and end of every other row until 27 (28, 28) sts remain. Bind off 2 sts at beg of each of the next 6 rows, then bind off remaining 15 (16, 16) sts.

Scarf: Cast on 185 (194, 194) sts. Work in pattern st for 7 inches. Bind off loosely in pattern.

Finishing: Sew side, sleeve and shoulder seams. Sew in sleeves. Work 2 rows of single crochet around the edge of the sleeves and the lower edge of the body and 1 row around the front and neck edges. Turn under the 1-inch hem on the sleeves and sew to the wrong side. Face the front edges with grosgrain ribbon. Cut into the ribbon under each buttonhole and finish the buttonholes with an overcast stitch. Sew on buttons. Block scarf, then face it with net material. Sew one end of scarf to neck edge 7 (7, 9) sts from the left front border, then continue sewing the scarf to the neck edge to within 7 (7, 9) sts of the right front border, leaving the right end of the scarf free. Tack the left tip of the scarf to the left front of the sweater with a button and form a loop for the insertion of the scarf end.

OPEN STRIPES

As shown on page 124

Design and directions courtesy of Emile Bernat & Sons Company

Directions for dress are written for small size (10–12). Changes for medium (14–16) and large (18–20) are in parentheses.

MATERIALS: Bernat Meadowspun: 10 (11, 13) 1-ounce skeins. Straight knitting needles No. 1, No. 2, and No. 3. Circular knitting needle No. 3. Steel crochet hook No. 2. 3 ¾-inch rings, 1 yard belting 1 inch wide, 2 snap fasteners.

GAUGE: 15 sts (2 lace patterns plus 1 p st) = 2 inches

Note: All increases and decreases are made in the p rib between the lace patterns.

Yoke: Starting at neck edge and using No. 1 needles, cast on 160 (176, 192) sts. Work back and forth in k 1, p 1 ribbing for 14 rows. Change to No. 2 needles and continue in ribbing for 11 rows more. Change to circular needle and continue to work back and forth in k 1, p 1 ribbing until piece measures 2½ inches. On the next row k and inc 1 st in each st—320 (352, 384) sts. Do not turn. Place a marker in work to mark beg of rnds, then join, being careful not to twist sts. **Rnd 1:** * P 1, k 2, yo, sl 1, k 2 tog, psso, yo, k 2, rep from * around. **Rnds 2, 4:** * P 1, k 7, rep from * around. **Rnd 3:** * P 1, k 2 tog, yo, k 3, yo, k 2 tog, rep from * around. Rep these 4 rnds 3 times more and end with Rnd 4. **1st Inc Rnd:** Starting at beg of rnd, * p the next st, inc 1 st in same st, k 2, yo, sl 1, k 2 tog, psso, yo, k 2, rep from * around—40 (44, 48) sts increased. Work even in new pattern for 11 (15, 19) rnds, ending with Rnd 4. **2nd Inc Rnd:** Starting at beg of the next rnd, * p 1, inc 1 st in next st, k 2, yo, sl 1, k 2 tog, psso, yo, k 2, rep from * around—40 (44, 48) sts increased. Work even in new pattern on 400 (440, 480) sts until piece measures 7½ (8, 8½) inches, ending with Rnd 2 or 4. *Divide Sts for Body and Sleeves:* Starting at beg of a rnd (back), work in pattern as established on the next 63 (73, 73) sts and sl these sts onto a holder to be worked later for half of back, then using No. 3 straight needles, work in pattern as established on next 77 (87, 97) sts for one sleeve. Leave remaining sts on the circular needle.

Sleeves: Cast on 13 sts, turn. **Row 1:** * K 3, p 7, rep from * and end p 7. **Row 2:** Cast on 13 sts, turn, * p 3, work in lace pattern as established on next 7 sts, rep from * and end p 3. **Row 3:** K 3, * P 7, k 3, rep from * across row. **Row 4:** P 3, * work next 7 sts in lace pattern, p 3, rep from * across row. Work back and forth in pattern as established now until piece measures 1 (1¼, 1½) inches above the cast-on sts, ending with a wrong side row. On the next row dec 1 st in each p 3 rib—11 (12, 13) sts decreased. Continue in new pattern until piece measures 2 (2½, 3) inches, ending with a wrong side row. On the next row dec 1 st in each p 2 rib—11 (12, 13) sts decreased. Change to No. 1 needles now and k 1, p 1 in ribbing on 81 (89, 97) sts for 1 inch. Bind off. With right side of work facing, join yarn at underarm and work next 123 (133, 143) sts for front and sl these sts onto another holder. Work next 77 (87, 97) sts for other sleeve, leave remaining sts on the circular needle. Finish 2nd sleeve to correspond to 1st sleeve. Sew sleeve seams.

Body: With right side of work facing you, join yarn at underarm, and work across 60 (60, 70) remaining sts of back. Being sure that the yoke opening is at back, work across 63 (73, 73) sts on holder, pick up and k 27 sts across the underarm, then work 123 (133, 143) sts of front and pick up 27 sts for other underarm. Continue around and around in pattern now as established on 300 (320, 340) sts until dress is desired length. Bind off.

Finishing: Sew center back seam of yoke. Work 3 rows of single crochet around the lower edge of the dress. Steam dress lightly. *Belt:* Using No. 1 needles, cast on 20 sts. Work even in stockinette st for desired length. Bind off. *Buckle:* Single crochet around 1 ring, add 2nd ring and single crochet around, then add 3rd ring and work in the same manner. Fold belt in half lengthwise, using the p side for the right side and seam. Line belt with belting, if desired. Sew one end of belt over 1 ring. Sew snap fasteners at other end for secure closing of belt.

ELEGANCE
As shown on page 125

Design and directions courtesy of Emile Bernat & Sons Company

Directions for dress are written for small size (10–12). Changes for medium (14–16) and large (18–20) are in parentheses.

MATERIALS: Bernat Meadowspun: 18 (19, 20) 1-ounce balls. Straight knitting needles No. 3. Steel crochet hook No. 00.

GAUGE: 13 sts and 17 rows = 2 inches

PATTERN STITCH:

Row 1: K 1, * yo, k 2, sl 1, k 1, psso, k 3, yo, sl 1, k 1, psso, rep from * across.
Row 2 and All Even Rows: P.
Rows 3, 5, 7, 9, 11: K 1, * yo, k 2, sl 1, k 1, psso, k 2 tog, k 2, yo, k 1, rep from * across.
Row 13: K 1, * k 1, yo, k 1, sl 1, k 1, psso, k 2 tog, k 1, yo, k 2, rep from * across.
Row 15: K 1, * k 2, yo, sl 1, k 1, psso, k 2 tog, yo, k 3, rep from * across.
Row 17: K 2 tog, * k 2, yo, sl 1, k 1, psso, yo, k 2, sl 1, k 1, psso, k 1, rep from * and end k 2, yo, sl 1, k 1, psso, yo, k 4.
Rows 19, 21, 23, 25, 27: K 2 tog, * k 2, yo, k 1, yo, k 2, sl 1, k 1, psso, k 2 tog, rep from * and end k 1 instead of k 2 tog.
Row 29: K 2 tog, * k 1, yo, k 3, yo, k 1, sl 1, k 1, psso, k 2 tog, rep from * and end k 1, instead of k 2 tog.

Row 31: K 2 tog, * yo, k 5, yo, sl 1, k 1, psso, k 2 tog, rep from * and end k 1, instead of k 2 tog.
Row 32: P.

Repeat these 32 rows for pattern stitch. *Note:* This dress has been planned for 38½ (39½, 40½)-inch finished length to start of shoulder shaping. If you wish your dress to be longer or shorter, work more or fewer inches before the start of the armhole shaping.

Back: Cast on 118 (127, 136) sts. Work even in pattern st until 8 patterns (256 rows) have been completed, ending with Row 32. *Yoke:* Rep Rows 1 and 2, then rep Rows 3 and 4 only for yoke pattern 4 (6, 8) times more. *Shape Armholes:* Bind off 6 sts at beg of each of the next 2 rows, then dec 1 st at beg and end of every other row 7 times, ending with a p row— 92 (101, 110) sts. Work now as follows: **Row 1:** K 1, k 2 tog, k 2, yo, k 1, * yo, k 2, sl 1, k 1, psso, k 2 tog, k 2, yo, k 1, rep from * and end yo, k 2, sl 1, k 1, psso, k 1. **Row 2:** P. Rep these 2 rows until armholes measure 7¼ (7¾, 8¼) inches. *Shape Shoulders:* Bind off 6 (7, 8) sts at beg of each of the next 8 rows. Bind off remaining 44 (45, 46) sts.

Front: Work to correspond to back until armholes measure 4¾ (5¼, 5¾) inches, ending with a p row—92 (101, 110) sts.

Shape Neck: Work 37 (41, 45) sts, join another ball of yarn and bind off center 18 (19, 20) sts, then work to end of row. Working on both sides at same time, dec 1 st at each neck edge every row 8 times, then every other row 5 times. Work even on 24 (28, 32) sts of each side until armholes measure 7¼ (7¾, 8¼) inches. *Shape Shoulders:* Bind off 6 (7, 8) sts at each arm edge 4 times.

Sleeves: Cast on 46 (46, 55) sts. Rep Rows 3 and 4 of pattern st for 1 inch. On the next row inc 1 st at beg and end of row and rep this inc every 6th row 15 (17, 17) times more, forming new patterns as sts are increased. Work even now on 78 (82, 91) sts until entire piece measures 16½ inches. *Shape Cap:* Bind off 6 sts at beg of each of the next 2 rows, then dec 1 st at beg and end of every other row for 4¼ (4¾, 5¼) inches. Bind off 3 (3, 4) sts at beg of each of the next 6 rows. Bind off remaining sts.

Finishing: Sew side, shoulder and sleeve seams. Sew in sleeves. *Edging:* **Rnd 1:** Join yarn at right shoulder seam and work in single crochet around the neck edge, join with a sl st at end of rnd. **Rnd 2:** Chain 2, work 1 double crochet in each st, join with a sl st. Fasten off. Press piece lightly.

TEN

Tatting Directions

HOW TO TAT

Tatting designs are composed of a series of rings and picots. The rings form the base of the design and the picots are used for joining the motifs and for decoration. A shuttle is the implement used in the practice of the art. Before starting the actual work it is necessary to wind the thread to be used around the bobbin in the center of the shuttle, first inserting the thread through the hole in the center of the bobbin and tying a knot to secure it in place, then winding the thread around, being careful that it does not extend beyond the edge of the shuttle, and leaving approximately a 12-inch length extending beyond the wound shuttle. The double stitch is the basic tatting stitch.

THE DOUBLE STITCH

STEP 1

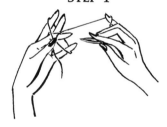

Hold the end of the thread between the thumb and forefinger of the left hand and the shuttle in the right hand, then pass the thread around the fingers of the left hand, bring it back and pass it between the thumb and forefinger, which now holds both threads. Being sure that the thread is held loosely enough so that it will slide easily between the fingers of the left hand, let the end of it fall inside the hand, and pass the thread from the shuttle around the little finger of the right hand.

STEP 2

Bring the shuttle under the thread stretched from the little finger of the right hand from right to left under the thread stretched between the forefinger and the middle finger of the left hand.

STEP 3

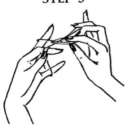

Return the shuttle over the thread from left to right, release the thread from the little finger of the right hand, lower the middle finger of the left hand to release the tension, draw the shuttle thread taut, then slowly raise the middle finger, thus sliding the loop formed into position between the thumb and forefinger and completing the first half of the

double stitch. Notice as you work that the shuttle thread is encircled by a loose loop made by the circle of thread in the left hand. It is very important that the shuttle thread is held taut until this loop is in position.

STEP 4

To work the second part of the double stitch, bring the shuttle back over the thread held between the middle and forefinger of the left hand, then under that thread with the right hand stretching the thread while the middle finger of the left hand bends and then lifts, thus sliding the loop into position as before and completing the second part of the double stitch.

PICOTS

Picots in tatting, used for joining the ring motifs and for decoration, are made after the completion of at least two double stitches. They are made by leaving a free loop above the thread held taut while making the first part of the next double stitch, leaving a little space between the knots, and then completing the second half of the next double stitch. The number of picots for a particular design are always given in the directions.

JOINING RINGS

When the required number of stitches have been made for a particular ring, form the ring by picking up with a crochet hook the thread around the fingers of the left hand and inserting it into the picot where it is to be joined. The loop formed in this way should be large enough to pass the shuttle through; be careful not to twist the loop while doing this. When the shuttle has been passed through, stretch the circular thread once more, being certain that it slides easily before continuing on with your work.

When a new thread is required to go on with the work, make a square knot close to the base of the last ring. The knot will prevent the ring from being "drawn up," and

should be cut off after a few more stitches have been worked.

When directions call for reversing your work, this effect is achieved by turning the previous ring over so that the base of it is at the top when starting a new ring. *Note:* All completed rings should be held to the left of the ring in work.

When a particular design calls for the use of two shuttles, as in a design where the little rings are not to be connected at the base of the thread, or when the passage of thread from one group of stitches to another is to be concealed, start by joining the ends of two threads with a knot. The left hand then holds the thread of the auxiliary shuttle wound twice around the fourth finger, leaving the shuttle hanging free. Work with the first shuttle (on the right) only. It is the thread held in the right hand that constitutes the foundation thread, and the one on the left that forms the desired pattern.

Abbreviations

beg	beginning
ch	chain stitch
ds	double stitch
d tr c	double treble crochet
kn	knot
p	picot
rep	repeat
rw	reverse work
sc	single crochet
sl st	slip stitch
sp	space
tr c	treble crochet
*	indicates directions following are to be repeated as necessary

SMALL FLOWERS

As shown on page 98

Design and directions courtesy of D.M.C. Corporation

MATERIALS: D.M.C. Pearl Cotton, Art. 116, or Crochet Cotton Cordonnet, Art. 151. Tatting shuttle. Steel crochet hook No. 9.

Center: Make a ring of 12 p each separated by 2 ds. Beginning with 1 ds and ending with 1 ds, close, knot, and cut the threads. *Small Flowers:* (Make 6): Work 4 small rings, each consisting of 6 ds, 1 p and 6 ds and close, bringing the rings close together. Attach each flower to the 2nd p of the center ring and join one flower to the next through the p's which are adjacent.

DELICATE TRACERY

As shown on page 98

Design and directions courtesy of D.M.C. Corporation

MATERIALS: D.M.C. Pearl Cotton Art. 116, or Crochet Cotton Cordonnet, Art. 151. Tatting Shuttle. Steel crochet hook No. 9.

Center: Make 4 rings of 8 ds, 1 p, 8 ds, 1 p, and 8 ds. Close each one and bring them together in the middle. Knot and cut off the threads. *Border Around Center:* Make 12 rings of 5 ds and 5 p separated by 2 ds and 5 ds, close. Join the 1st ring to the nearest p of the center ring, leaving a length of thread and after having closed the ring, leave the same space interval before making the second ring, joining that ring to the next p of the center. In finishing, join the last ring to the 1st one. To form the strip of

lace, place as many motifs as necessary for desired length horizontally next to each other, joining them at adjacent p points. For desired width, place horizontal strips one above the other, filling the centers between with motif centers only and joining all strips and motif centers at adjacent p points. For top of edging make as many groups of 3 rings as necessary, the 1st ring composed of 24 ds with 2 p and the remaining 2 of 6 ds, 1 p, 6 ds, 1 p and 6 ds. Make a crocheted edge at the top of the strip if desired by working * 1 tr c in the top p of a flower, 8 ch, 1 sl st in the p of the 1st ring of a triangle, 6 ch, 1 sl st in the following p, 8 ch, rep from *across.

CLOVERLEAF

As shown on page 99

Design and directions courtesy of D.M.C. Corporation

MATERIALS: D.M.C. Pearl Cotton, Art. 116, or Crochet Cotton Cordonnet, Art. 151. Tatting shuttle. Steel crochet hook No. 1.

Rings: Tie two shuttle threads together. Work 1 small ring of 7 ds, 5 p separated by 2 ds and 3 dc, close. Work 1 large ring now of 3 ds, attach to last p of previous ring, then work 8 p separated by 2 ds, 3 ds, close. Work now 1 small ring of 3 ds. Attach to last p of previous ring, work 4 p separated by 2 ds, 7 ds and close. Rw, then with the 2nd thread work one loop of 6 ds, 1 large p and 6 ds, thus forming the stem. Rep 3 times now from the beginning, but instead of the 1st p of the 1st ring, attach piece to the last p of the preceding group. For the arch, attach piece after the 6th ds in the long p that forms center of design.

DAINTY FLOWERS AND LACE
As shown on page 100

Design and directions courtesy of American Thread Company

MATERIALS: Gem Mercerized Cotton, size 30. Tatting shuttle. Steel crochet hook No. 11.

Rings: (Make 5): 6 ds, p, 6 ds, close. * Turn. Ch, 6 ds, 3 p separated by 2 ds, 6 ds, p, 6 ds, join to p of the 4th ring made, 4 ds, turn. **Next Ring:** 2 ds, 7 p separated by 2 ds, 2 ds, close, turn. Ch, 4 ds, p, 6 ds, join to p on the opposite ch, 6 ds, 3 p separated by 2 ds, 6 ds, turn. **Next Ring:** 6 ds, p, 6 ds, close. **Next Ring:** 6 ds, join to p of ch, 6 ds, close. Work 3 more rings of 6 ds, p and 6 ds, then rep from * for desired length.

MILLE FLEURS
As shown on page 100

Design and directions courtesy of American Thread Company

MATERIALS: Gem Mercerized Cotton, size 30. Tatting shuttle. Steel crochet hook No. 11.

Rings: 3 ds, 3 p separated by 3 ds, 3 ds, close. Ch, 4 ds, 3 p separated by 4 ds, 4 ds, * join to center p of ring, 4 ds, turn. **Next Ring:** 1 ds, 8 p separated by 1 ds, 1 ds, close, turn. Ch, 4 ds, turn. **Next Ring:**

3 ds, 3 p separated by 3 ds, 3 ds, close, turn. Ch, 4 ds, join to p on opposite ch, 4 ds, p, 4 ds, p, 4 ds, rep from * for desired length.

FALLING SNOWFLAKES
As shown on page 100

Design and directions courtesy of American Thread Company

MATERIALS: Gem Mercerized Cotton, size 30. Tatting shuttle. Steel crochet hook No. 11.

Rings: 4 ds, p, 4 ds, p, 4 ds, p, 4 ds, close. **Next Ring:** 4 ds, join to last p of last ring, 4 ds, p, 2 ds, p, 2 ds, p, 4 ds, p, 4 ds, close. **Next Ring:** 4 ds, join to last p of last ring, 4 ds, p, 4 ds, p, 4 ds, close. Rep from beg once, ** turn. Ch, 8 ds, p, 3 ds, p, 3 ds, p, 8 ds, p, 8 ds, join to center p of last large ring, 8 ds, turn. **Next Ring:** 2 ds, 6 p separated by 2 ds, 2 ds, close. Join to last p of ring just completed. **Next Ring:** 3 ds, p, 3 ds, join to free p of last clover made, 3 ds, p, 3 ds, close. Join to 2nd p of center ring. **Next Ring:** 3 ds, join to side p of last small ring, 3 ds, p, 3 ds, p, 3 ds, close. * Join to next p of center ring. **Next Ring:** 3 ds, join to side p of last small ring, 3 ds, p, 3 ds, p, 3 ds, close. Rep from * 3 times, turn. Ch, 8 ds, p, 8 ds, join to single p on opposite ch, 8 ds, p, 3 ds, p, 3 ds, p, 8 ds, turn. **Next Ring:** 4 ds, p, 4 ds, p, 4 ds, p, 4 ds, close. **Next Ring:** 4 ds, join to last p of last ring made, 4 ds, p, 2 ds, join to single p of last ch, 2 ds, p, 4 ds, p, 4 ds, close. **Next Ring:** 4 ds, join to last p of last ring made, 4 ds, join to center p of last small ring group,

4 ds, p, 4 ds, close. **Next Ring:** 4 ds, join to last p of last ring, 4 ds, p, 4 ds, p, 4 ds, close. **Next Ring:** 4 ds, join to last p of last ring, 4 ds, 3 p separated by 2 ds, 4 ds, p, 4 ds, close. **Next Ring:** 4 ds, join to last p of last ring, 4 ds, p, 4 ds, p, 4 ds, close. Turn. Rep from ** for length desired.

SCALLOPED LACE
As shown on page 101

Design and directions courtesy of American Thread Company

MATERIALS: Gem Mercerized Cotton, size 30. Tatting shuttle. Steel crochet hook No. 11.

Scallop: Rings: 3 ds, 5 p separated by 3 ds, 3 ds, close, turn, leave 1/8 inch space. **Next Ring:** 3 ds, long p, 3 ds, small p, 6 ds, close, turn, * leave 1/8 inch space. **Next Ring:** 3 ds, join to last p of large ring, 3 ds, 4 p separated by 3 ds, 3 ds, close, leave 1/8 inch space. **Next Ring:** 6 ds, p, 6 ds, close, turn. Rep from *, leave 1/8 inch space. Work 3 large rings joining in same manner as other large rings, turn. Leave 1/8 inch space. **Next Ring:** 6 ds, join to p of last small ring, 6 ds, close, turn. Leave 1/8 inch space. **Next Ring:** 3 ds, join to p of large ring, 3 ds, 4 p separated by 3 ds, 3 ds, close, turn. Work 2 large rings joining them in same manner as other large rings, turn. Leave 1/8 inch space. **Next Ring:** 6 ds, join to joining of last 2 small rings, 6 ds, close, turn. Leave 1/8 inch space. **Next Ring:** 3 ds, join to large ring, 3 ds, 4 p separated by 3 ds, 3 ds, close, turn. Leave 1/8 inch

space. **Next Ring:** 6 ds, join to p of corresponding ring, 6 ds, close, turn. Leave 1/8 inch space. **Next Ring:** 3 ds, join to last p of last ring, 3 ds, 4 p separated by 3 ds, 3 ds, close, turn. Leave 1/8 inch space. **Next Ring:** 6 ds, join the small p of opposite ring, 3 ds, long p, 3 ds, close ring, leave 1/8 inch space. Work 1 more ring joining to large ring, cut thread.

Top Joining: Work a 2nd scallop, joining it to the 1st scallop at center p of 3 large rings. Work as many scallops as needed for desired length. Join thread in 1st p of large ring and with a crochet hook, ch 3, sc in p of small ring, ch 3, sc in p of next small ring, ch 3, sc in p of next large ring, ch 3, rep from beg across the straight edge of the scallops.

CLOUDS
As shown on page 102

Design and directions courtesy of D.M.C. Corporation

MATERIALS: D.M.C. Pearl Cotton, Art. 116, or Crochet Cotton Cordonnet, Art. 151. Tatting shuttle. Steel crochet hook No. 9.

Center Portion: 9 ds, 1 p, 8 ds, 1 p, 9 ds, close. **Next Ring:** 9 ds, attach to p of previous ring, 4 ds, attach to p of the circle on previous ring, 4 ds, 1 p, 9 ds, close. **Next Ring:** 9 ds, attach to previous ring, 4 ds, attach to last p of preceding ring, 4 ds, 1 p, 9 ds, close. Make 4 other rings in this manner attaching them together only at the side.

Tie a 2nd thread to the starting thread. When the 7 rings have been made, work as follows: Rw on the 2nd thread. For one arch at the bottom work 14 ds, rw. With the 1st thread make a ring of 12 ds, attach to p on the last ring of the center portion, 5 ds, 1 p, 9 ds, close. Rw. For the 2nd arch on the opposite side make a ring in the same manner as the 1st and attach it to the loop that precedes the center. Passing the 2nd thread underneath now, make 10 ds, 1 p, 10 ds, 1 p, 5 ds, 1 p, and 10 ds. Make all centers in this way.

Rings at Top of Center: 10 ds, attach to top of the 4th ring of center, 5 ds, attach to p of the 6th ring of the following center. Rw. Make another ring, but reversed for the ds and the p's. Rw. With the 2nd thread, work 10 ds, attach to the next free center portion, 10 ds, attach to the top p of the 2nd ring. Rw. Work one arch of 18 ds with a p after the 9th ds.

Crochet Edging at Top and Bottom: * Work 1 sl st in the nearest p, ch 9, 1 sl st in the following p, rep from * for desired length.

FLORAL FANTASY

As shown on page 103

Design and directions courtesy of D.M.C. Corporation

MATERIALS: D.M.C. Pearl Cotton, Art. 116, or Crochet Cotton Cordonnet, Art. 151. Tatting shuttle. Steel crochet hook No. 9.

Rings: Make a center ring of 8 p, each

separated by 2 ds between, then fasten with a knot in the 1st p without cutting the thread. *Side Rings:* (Make 8): 3 ds, 7 p separated by 2 ds, and 3 ds, close. Join with a knot in one p of the center ring, leaving the thread loose. The balance of the 8 side rings are made by joining to the last p of the preceding ring instead of working the 1st p. The last ring is joined to the 1st by the last p. The group of as many completed rings as desired is joined by linking 2 rings of one completed ring to 2 rings of an adjacent one.

This insertion may be used as shown or finished additionally at top and bottom with a series of crocheted tr c and ch sts, working the tr c's into p's as they occur and working a number of ch in between so that work lies flat.

FLOWER FROST

As shown on page 108

Design and directions courtesy of Coats & Clark, Inc. Doily measures 16 inches in diameter.

MATERIALS: Clark's Big Ball Mercerized Crochet, Art. B.34, size 30: 2 balls; or Art. B.345: 1 ball. Tatting shuttle. Steel crochet hook No. 9.

Rnd 1: Make a ring of 8 ds, 3 p separated by 3 ds, 8 ds, close. Make a (ring of 8 ds, join to last p of previous ring, 3 ds, 2 p separated by 3 ds, 8 ds, close) 7 times, join last ring to 1st ring. Tie and cut.
Rnd 2: Tie threads together and attach to p of any ring of previous rnd, * ch of 6 ds, p, 6 ds, join to p of next ring, rep from

* around. Tie and cut. **Rnd 3:** Tie threads as before and attach to p of any ch of previous rnd, * ch of 8 ds, 2 p separated by 8 ds, 8 ds, join to p of next ch, rep from * around. Tie and cut. **Rnd 4:** *1st Motif:* Tie threads. Make a ring of 8 ds, p, 3 ds, p, 8 ds, close. Rw, make a ch of 3 ds, 3 p separated by 3 ds, 3 ds. Rw, make a ring of 8 ds, join to last p of previous ring, 3 ds, p, 8 ds, close. Rw, make a ch of 3 ds, p, 3 ds, join to last p of 1st ch of previous rnd, 3 ds, p, 3 ds. Rw, make a ring as before, joining to previous ring. Rw, ch as before, join to 1st p of next ch. (Rw, ring as before, join to previous ring. Rw, make a ch of 3 ds, 3 p separated by 3 ds and 3 ds) 5 times and join last ring to 1st ring and last ch at base of 1st ring (motif made). Tie and cut. * Tie threads together, make a ring of 8 ds, p, 3 ds, p, 8 ds, close. Rw, make a ch of 3 ds, p, 3 ds, join to center p of 4th ch of previous motif, 3 ds, p, 3 ds. Rw, make a ring of 8 ds, join to last p of previous ring, 3 ds, p, 8 ds, close. Rw, ch as before, join to last p of same ch of previous rnd. Rw, make a ring as before, join to previous ring. Rw, ch as before, join to 1st p of next ch of previous rnd and complete motif as before. There are no more joinings. Tie and cut. Rep from * 6 times more, then join last motif to 1st motif. Tie and cut 8 motifs. **Rnd 5:** Tie threads as before, make a ring of 8 ds, p, 3 ds, p, 8 ds, close. Rw, make a ch of 3 ds, p, 3 ds, join to center p of 5th ch of 3 ds, p, 3 ds, join to center p of 5th ch of 1st motif, 3 ds, p, 3 ds. Rw, make a

ring of 8 ds, join to last p of previous ring, 3 ds, p, 8 ds, close. Rw, ch as before, join to center p of 8th ch of next motif. (Rw, make a ring as before, join to previous ring. Rw, make a ch of 3 ds, 3 p separated by 3 ds and 3 ds) 4 times, join last ch to base of 1st ring (small motif). Tie and cut. (Tie threads together, make a ring of 8 ds, p, 3 ds, p, 8 ds, close. Rw, make a ch of 3 ds, p, 3 ds, skip 2 ch on same motif of previous rnd and join to center p of next ch, 3 ds, p, 3 ds. Rw, make a ring as before and join as before. Rw, make a ch as before, join to center p of adjacent ch of next motif of previous rnd and complete as before. Tie and cut.) 7 times. **Rnd 6:** Tie threads, make a ring of 8 ds, p, 8 ds, close. Rw, make a long ch of 8 ds, 2 p separated by 8 ds, 6 ds, then make a ring of 8 ds, p, 3 ds, p, 8 ds, close. Reversing curve of chain now, make a ch of 3 ds, p, 3 ds, join to p of next-to-last ring, 3 ds, p, 3 ds. Rw, make a ring as before, join to previous ring. Rw, make a ch of 3 ds, p, 3 ds, join to center p of 3rd ch of 1st small motif of previous rnd, 3 ds, p, 3 ds, * (Rw, make a ring, join as before. Rw, ch as before, join to center p of next ch of motif of next-to-last rnd) twice. Rw, make a ring, join as before, rw, make a ch as before, join to center p of next ch of next small motif of previous rnd. Rw, make a ring, join as before. Rw, make a ch of 3 ds, 3 p separated by 3 ds and 3 ds. Rw, make a ring of 8 ds, join to last p of previous ring, 3 ds, join to p of 1st ring, 8 ds, close. Reversing curve of chain now, make a long ch of 6 ds, join to last p of previous long ch, 8 ds, p, 8 ds. Rw, make a ring of 8 ds, join to center p of next-to-last ch, 8 ds, close. Make a ring as before, join to center p of next ch of same small motif of previous rnd. Rw, make a ch of 8 ds, p and 8 ds. Rw, make a small ring of 4 ds, join to last p of same ch, 4 ds, close. Make a small ring as before, join to 1st p of next ch. Rw and ch as before. Rw, make a ring of 8 ds, join to center p of same ch, 8 ds, close. Make a ring of 8 ds, p, 8 ds, close. Rw, make a long ch of 8 ds, 2 p separated by 8 ds and 6 ds. Make a ring of 8 ds, p, 3 ds, p, 8 ds, close. Reversing curve of chain now, make a ch of 3 ds, p, 3 ds, join to p of next-to-last ring, 3 ds, p and 3 ds. Rw, make a ring as before, join to previous ring. Rw, make a ch of 3 ds, p, 3 ds, join to center p of next ch of same small motif of previous rnd, 3 ds, p and 3 ds. Rep from * around. Tie and cut. **Rnd 7:** Tie threads together, make a small ring of 4 ds, join to free p of any ch of previous rnd, 4 ds, close. * Rw, make a ch of 8 ds, p and 8 ds. Rw, make a small ring as before, join to same p. Rw, make a ch as before. Rw, make a small ring, join to next free p. Rep from * around and end with ch, join at base of 1st small ring. Tie and cut. **Rnds 8, 9:** Tie threads together, make a small ring of 4 ds, join to p of 1st ch of previous rnd, 4 ds, close. * Rw, make a ch of 8 ds, p and 8 ds. Rw, make a small ring as before, join to same p. Rw, make a ch as before. Rw, skip next free p, make a small ring and join to next free p. Rep

from * around and join as before. Tie and cut. **Rnd 10:** Tie threads, make a small ring of 4 ds, join to p of 1st ch of previous rnd, 4 ds, close. * Rw, make a ch of 8 ds, p, 8 ds. Rw, make a small ring as before, join to same p. Rw, make a ch of 2 ds, p and 2 ds. Rw, make a small ring, join to next free p. Rep from * around and end with a ch of 2 ds, p and 2 ds, join at base of 1st small ring. Tie and cut. **Rnd 11:** Tie threads, make a ring of 8 ds, p, 3 ds, p, 8 ds, close. Rw, make a ch of 3 ds, p and 3 ds, join to p of 1st ch of previous rnd, 3 ds, p, 3 ds. (Rw, make a ring of 8 ds, join to previous ring, 3 ds, p, 8 ds, close. Rw, ch of 3 ds, 3 p separated by 3 ds and 3 ds) 7 times, join last ch at base of 1st ring. Tie and cut. * Tie threads together, make a ring of 8 ds, p, 3 ds, p, 8 ds, close. Rw, make a ch of 3 ds, p, 3 ds, skip next ch on previous motif and join to center p of next ch, 3 ds, p and 3 ds. Rw, make a ring of 8 ds, join to previous ring, 3 ds, p, 8 ds, close. Rw, make a ch of 3 ds, 3 p separated by 3 ds and 3 ds. Rw, make a ring as before, join to previous ring. Rw, make a ch of 3 ds, p, 3 ds, skip next free p's on previous ring. Rw, make a ch of 3 ds, p, 3 ds, skip next free p's on previous rnd and join to next free p, 3 ds, p and 3 ds. Rw, and complete motif as before, no more joinings. Tie and cut. Rep from * around, joining last motif to 1st motif (32 motifs). Tie and cut. Starch piece lightly and press.

Acknowledgments

The author is most grateful to the yarn companies listed below for their complete cooperation in the compilation of the pattern portion of this book and for their effort in maintaining the high standards of needlework art today. Credit for each of the designs is given along with the pattern instructions given for them.

American Thread Company, Stamford, Connecticut
Emile Bernat & Sons Co., Uxbridge, Massachusetts
Brunswick Worsted Mills, Inc., Pickens, South Carolina
Coats & Clark, Inc., New York, New York
D.M.C. Corporation, Elizabeth, New Jersey
Reynolds Yarns, Inc., Hauppauge, New York
Scovill Manufacturing Company, New York, New York
Bernhard Ulmann Company, Long Island City, New York
William Unger & Co. Inc., New York, New York

Bibliography

Beebe, Mrs. C., *Lace, Ancient and Modern.* New York: Sharps Publishing Co., 1880.

Blum, Clara M., *Old World Lace.* New York: E. P. Dutton & Co., 1920.

Brooke, Margaret L., *Lace in the Making.* London: G. Routledge & Sons, Ltd., 1923.

Caplin, Jessie F., *The Lace Book.* New York: Macmillan Co., 1932.

Chronicle of the Museum for the Arts of Decoration of the Cooper Union, Vol. I, No. 11. New York: Cooper-Hewitt Museum, 1945.

Ciga Magazine, No. 1, 1973, *Lace of the Mermaids.* Venice, Italy, 1973.

Close, Eunice, *Lace Making.* London: John Gifford, Ltd., 1970.

de Dillmont, T., *Encyclopedia of Needlework.* Mulhouse, France: D.M.C. Library, 1971.

Encyclopaedia Britannica. Chicago: University of Chicago, 1943.

Head, Mrs. R. E., *The Lace and Embroidery Collector.* New York: Dodd, Mead & Co., 1922.

Henneberg, Alfred, Freiherr von, *The Art and Craft of Old Lace.* New York: E. Weyhe, 1931.

Jones, Mary Eirwen, *The Romance of Lace.* London: Staples Press, 1951.

Kellogg, Mrs. Charlotte (Hoffman), *Bobbins of Belgium.* New York: Funk & Wagnalls, 1920.

Legion d'Honneur Magazine, Napoleon Lace. Paris.

Lowes, Emily Leigh, *Chats on Old Lace and Needlework*. London: T. F. Unwin, 1919.

Mayer, Christa C., "Lace and the Male Ego," in *Antiques Magazine*, January–February, 1968.

———— "Three Centuries of Bobbin Lace," in *Antiques Magazine*, August, 1966.

———— "Two Centuries of Needle Lace," in *Antiques Magazine*, February, 1965.

Moore, Hannah Hudson, *The Lace Book*. New York: F. A. Stokes Co., 1904.

Palliser, Fanny Marryat, *History of Lace*. New York: C. Scribner's Sons, 1902.

Pethebridge, Jeanette E., *A Manual of Lace*. London: Cassell, 1947.

Powys, Marian, *Lace and Lace-Making*. Kent, England: C. T. Branford, 1953.

Sharp, A. Mary, *Point and Pillow Lace*. London: J. Murray, 1899.

Techy, Margaret, *Filet Crochet Lace*. New York: Harper & Bros., 1943.

Index